THE FOUNDATIONS
OF THE THEOLOGY
OF JUDAISM

THE FOUNDATIONS OF THE THEOLOGY OF JUDAISM

Volume I

GOD

Jacob Neusner

JASON ARONSON INC.
Northvale, New Jersey
London

The Foundations of the Theology of Judaism

Volume I: God
Volume II: Torah
Volume III: Israel

Library of Congress Cataloging-in-Publication Data

Neusner, Jacob, 1932–
    The foundations of the theology of Judaism / Jacob Neusner.
      p. cm.
    Includes index.
    Contents : v. 1. God.
    ISBN 0-87668-738-9 (set). — ISBN 0-87668-737-0 (v. 1)
    1. Judaism—Doctrines. I. Title.
BM601.N484 1991
296.3—dc20   90-1122

Manufactured in the United States of America. Jason Aronson Inc. offers books and cassettes. For information and catalog write to Jason Aronson Inc., 230 Livingston Street, Northvale, New Jersey 07647.

For
my Talmud-haver of 1954–1957 and friend of my youth,
Rabbi Neil Gillman
of The Jewish Theological Seminary of America,
in these pages giving back to him what is his.

CONTENTS

PREFACE

Judaism knows God through the Torah. We know about God exactly what God has told us and what our sages of blessed memory have handed on from the revelation at Sinai to our own day as the truth, the tradition, about God. In this book I provide an account of what we know about God in the part of the Torah that is oral. The Oral Torah comprises the Mishnah, the two Talmuds, and the dozen or so Midrash-compilations that were completed in the formative age, the first seven centuries of the Common Era, in the Land of Israel and in Babylonia. In these pages we follow the account of God that our sages of blessed memory received in dialogue with the Written Torah or Hebrew Scriptures and then handed on in the Oral Torah. What they set forth is not "religious experience" in general terms, but a very specific account of God and what, through the Torah, we know.

Putting matters in that way is somewhat misleading. As we shall see, in the first of the documents that make up the oral part of the Torah, the Mishnah, we may accurately speak of what we know about God. In later compilations, however, we no longer know only about God. We know God as more than a principle and a premise of being (such as philosophers know about God), and even as more than a presence (as pious people know about God through prayer). Rather, we know God as a person and, by the end of the Oral Torah, even as a fully embodied personality. So the story of God that we gain in the Oral Torah is the unfolding of the knowledge of God in the Torah.

As a matter of fact, our sages know God in four aspects: (1) principle or premise, that is, the one who created the world and gave the Torah; (2) presence, that is, supernatural being resident in the Temple and present where two or more persons engage in discourse concerning the Torah; (3) person, that is, the one to whom prayer is addressed; and (4) personality, a God we can know and make our model. When God emerges as a personality, God is represented as (1) being corporeal, (2) exhibiting traits of human emotions, and (3) doing deeds that women and men do, in the way they do them.

What we shall see is that God in the first document of the Oral Torah, which is the Mishnah and related writings, appears as principle or premise and also as presence; the God of Judaism is never merely the God that followers must invoke to explain how things got going and work as they do. In the next stage of the Oral Torah, represented by the Talmud of the Land of Israel and related writings, God is portrayed not only as principle and presence, but as a person. In the third and final stage, the Babylonian Talmud, God emerges as a fully exposed personality whom we can know and love. It goes without saying that, since for Judaism God is known through the Torah, our sages of blessed memory recognize no need to prove the existence of God. The Torah proves the existence of God, and the glories of the natural world demonstrate the workings of God in the world. What humanity must do is explore what it means to be "in our image, after our likeness," that is, to be "like God." The sages of the Torah then bear the task of setting forth, through the Oral Torah, precisely the answer to that question: how are we "in God's image," "after God's likeness," and what does that mean? That is what this volume explains, in their words.

I thank my editor at Jason Aronson Inc., Arthur Kurzweil, for his usual perspicacious editorial judgment, which I do not take for granted. For me he is an ideal editor, and I have much pleasure in working with him on one project after another.

I consulted Professor William Scott Green, University of Rochester, on the execution of this book, and once more I gained from him much first-rate editorial and scholarly counsel.

My monograph, *The Incarnation of God: The Character of Divinity in Formative Judaism* (Philadelphia: Fortress Press, 1988), and, for the Mishnah, my *Judaism as Philosophy: The Method and Message of the Mishnah* (Columbia: University of South Carolina Press, 1991), form the theoretical framework for this volume on God in the theology of Judaism. This approach to the history of the unfolding of the Judaism of the dual Torah is spelled out in great detail in a number of other books of mine, among which the following will prove most readily accessible: *The Foundations of Judaism* (Philadelphia: Fortress, 1988); *Vanquished Nation, Broken Spirit: The Virtues of the Heart in Formative Judaism* (New York: Cambridge University Press, 1987); *Judaism in the Matrix of Christianity* (Philadelphia: Fortress Press, 1986); *Judaism and Christianity in the Age of Constantine: Issues of the Initial Confrontation* (Chicago: University of Chicago Press, 1987); *Death and Birth of Judaism: The Impact of Christianity, Secularism, and the Holocaust on Jewish Faith* (New York: Basic Books, 1987); and *Self-Fulfilling Prophecy: Exile and Return in the History of Judaism* (Boston: Beacon Press, 1987; 2nd printing: Atlanta: Scholars Press for South Florida Studies in the History of Judaism, 1990).

I owe thanks to three agencies. During the year in which I edited this book I was supported in part by a senior fellowship of the National Endowment for the Humanities (FA 28396-89), and I take much pride in offering my very hearty thanks to that agency for the recognition and material support that the fellowship afforded me. I found the NEH, particularly the Division of Fellowships and Seminars, always helpful and courteous in dealing with my application, and I must express my admiration and appreciation to that thoroughly professional staff of public servants. Second, Brown University augmented that fellowship with substantial funds to make it possible for me to spend the academic year 1989–1990 in full-time research. In my twenty-two years at Brown University, now concluded, I enjoyed the university's generous support for every research initiative that I undertook, and it was a welcome challenge to be worthy of the unusual opportunities accorded to me as a research scholar at that university. I never took for granted the University's commitment of scarce resources to my work in particular, and I now express my thanks commensurate to that commitment. Finally, the Institute for Advanced Study, where I wrote this book, afforded a pleasant setting in which to pursue full-time research. I thank all those who made it so, particularly the members for 1989–1990.

Jacob Neusner

Graduate Research Professor of Religious Studies
University of South Florida, Tampa

PROLOGUE: THE TASKS OF THEOLOGY IN JUDAISM

T heology forms a mode of learning—a science—that varies with the subject and the setting of the learning. In Judaism in particular, the principal task of theology is to draw out and make explicit the normative statements of Torah—that is, the acknowledged sources of Judaism—and to learn how to renew discourse in accord with these norms. Specifically, it is to delineate the worldview shaped within the experience and aspirations of the community of Judaism and to perceive the world within that view, with the goal of making the sight of ages to come yet more perspicacious. Vision received, vision reformed, vision transmitted—these are the tasks of theology in Judaism.

It is a commonplace that halakhic statements are normative and that theological statements represent an individual's private opinion. However, this trilogy of the theology of Judaism at its foundations is meant to put sources on display in such a way as to restate the theological task as normative too. I want to show that within the communities of the faithful of Judaism, the theology of Judaism in regard to God, Torah, and Israel may be perceived as part of public discourse, not merely private opinion—a point to be stressed in Chapter 1. The first task is to state what it is that Judaism teaches, to define both its principal concerns and its methods of expressing its ideas.[1] The work of definition is to discover what it is that theology wishes to say. This descriptive task—the perception of the vision received—is theological in its purpose.

When we wish to define Judaism, we first have to locate and encompass the whole range of texts in the canon of Judaism, for to define a religion is to state the substance of its canon, that is, to spell out the ideas found in the canonical literature. Second, coming to grips with that range of canonical texts is an exercise in the exegesis of exegesis. That is, we have to know how these texts are correctly read and interpreted and why we read them in one way rather than in some other. The theologian has to explain how these texts have been so read as to be received as everywhere pertinent. For Judaism is a religion of great age and diversity. To uncover the fundament of ultimate conviction everywhere present, and to do so with full reverence for diversity in the history of Judaism—the Judaism of the Dual Torah, the only Judaism to have attained an authoritative position over centuries within the Jewish people—we have to look for what is ubiquitous. And doing that, I think, is the process and the method: Discerning how things are made to happen ubiquitously and consistently yields the rules which we may extract from the happening as well as the substantive convictions that lie behind the rules. For when we ask about process and method, our interest is not simply in formal traits but also in substantive ones. Axiomatic to the "how" of process and method is the "what" of substance,

---

[1]At this time, however, I do not wish to enter into issues of Judaic dogmatics, the restatement of available and required truths for the current age. To do such work now is premature. For a long time we were told that Judaism has no theology, and certainly no dogmas. While the dogma of dogma-less Judaism has passed away with the generation to whom it seemed an urgent and compelling proposition, it has left discourse about and within Judaism in disarray. There is a poverty of philosophical clarity and decisive expression amid a superfluity of conviction—too much believing, too small perspicacious construction. As one person put it, "There is no God, but Israel is God's sole and chosen people." Furthermore, dogmatics lays the groundwork for the exercise of advocacy and apologetic. That exercise is a work of mediation between culture and revelation, between where the people are and where Torah wishes them to be. It seems to me self-evident that, until we have a richer and more responsible conception of what it is that awaits both advocacy and mediation, that is, Torah or Judaism, formulation of dogmas for defense is unimportant.

the elements of worldview which generate both the process and the method.

At this stage in the work, it is not the task of the theologian to declare the truth. All Judaism holds that the truth is revealed in Torah. It therefore is to be discovered in Torah. The theologian has to locate that point, within the intellectual structure of the faith, at which discovery may take place. The work is to lay out the lines of the truth, the frontiers of Torah. Now if we take seriously the current commonplace proposition that Judaism is a way of life, we are not going to find it easy to choose those people whose way of life defines Judaism and reveals Torah. The diversity among Jews is too great. Some Jews do not see themselves as engaged in an essentially religious mode of being at all. Others, whom we shall have to call by a separate name, Judaists, do see themselves as participants in a religious mode of being, Judaism. These religious Jews are themselves diverse; their way of life is not uniform. Therefore, the sustained effort to uncover the fundament of the true faith by describing the way of life of the Judaists is fruitless. The status quo does not contain within itself the fundament of the true faith. If we attempted to turn the way of life into a statement of theology or a source for deeper meaning, the best we would gain is a statement of culture. If, on the other hand, we turn to historical descriptions of the "authentic" way of life of Judaism, such as the *Shulhan Arukh,* we are speaking not of the way of life of all of the living, but rather of a holy book which is part of a holy canon. We might, therefore, just as well turn to the canon. Or, to state matters more bluntly, Judaism is not going to be described by sociology; nevertheless it must be described and interpreted.[2]

So we have to find a way of reading the holy books congruent to

---

[2]Obviously, I cannot concede that Judaism is practiced today only by those who now carry out the teachings of Jewish law, for example, as summed up in the *Shulhan Arukh.* It does not seem to be descriptively valid since vast numbers of Jews also regard themselves, and are generally regarded as, Judaists who do not live in accord with all of the law of Judaism all the time or ever. The choice then is (1) to declare that Judaism has no halakhah, or (2) to declare that all who do not keep the halakhah are not Judaists. Both propositions seem to me factually so far from the truth as to have to be set aside. The problem explored here then becomes urgent and unavoidable.

both their character and our interest in them. It seems to me that
this requirement is met with two questions. First, *how* do these texts
convey their message? What do we learn from the way they say
things and the way in which people have learned to hear what they
say? Second, *what* do they say that is pertinent to living as a Judaist
today? That is, once the canonical text leaves its particular moment
of history and journeys beyond its specific context, it has to discover
new life in other contexts. The way it does so is through the urgent
work of exegesis: comparing the words of one text to the ways of
another world and finding modes of harmonization and mediation
between the two. The only way to do theology in Judaism is
through the ongoing encounter with the Torah. Doing theology is
not merely reciting or paraphrasing the words, but rather asking
how the texts convey their message and what they say that we can
use.

Now the theologian's work is not solely to explain how the
diverse texts have been made to speak. For the much more complex
work of generalization, the theologian requires information about
commonalities amid the diversities of exegesis, the exegesis of
exegesis, so to speak. The theologian, first, has to uncover the
processes and modes of thought. To know how a given text has
been received is interesting. To know how the methods of recep-
tion, transmission, interpretation, and application of that text
correspond to methods to be located in the reading of other texts is
to know something important: the deeper structure of the processes
of interpretation, the method within the diverse methods of the
received exegesis. What is available for this work of generalization,
it is clear, is what is common among exegetical techniques of diverse
and discrete documents, that is, how all of them are read, through
all times, and in all places.

Second, when we speak of times and places, we arouse the
interest of the historian of religions. For what do we know about
the exegesis of a text if we cannot describe the contexts of ideas and
visions in which that exegesis is done, the impulse and motivation
that determine the particular choices of the exegete? What was the
question that had to be answered in those times for those people?
It is not enough to wonder what we learn from hermeneutics, that
is, *how* people say things about the commonalities of faith; we also

have also to know *what,* under diverse circumstances, they wish to say: The *substance* matters as much as the method. Here is the point at which comparative and historical studies in religions come to the fore.

In the work of description not only does context play its part; so too does consideration of choice, that is to say, comparison. We must know what things people *might* have said in order to understand the things they *do* choose to say. So these two go together: (1) the consideration of formal language, mode of interpreting and applying the canon, and (2) the historian's analysis of the range of the choices selected for serious attention, the comparison of diverse contexts and expressions of a given continuum of religion or diverse religions.

There is yet a third kind of thinking about religions which is to be invoked: an interest in the larger concrete, social, and historical framework in which Judaism comes to particular expression and definition, an interest characteristic of historians. When we have some clear picture of the procedures and methods of exegesis of the texts and of the choices available and made, we have yet to link our results to that world of the Jewish people that took shape in these processes and out of these dynamics. That is why I stress the conception that, from document to document and age to age, people developed the Torah's encounter with God, moving, as we shall see, from a philosophical to a deeply religious response to God's insistence, through the Torah, upon the heart of humanity: "You shall love the Lord your God with all your heart, with all your soul, and with all your might."

There is an ecology of Judaism: a natural framework in which all elements interact with all other elements to form a stable, coherent, and whole system. For if Judaism is to be described as it has endured, it has to be described where it has endured: in the political-social and imaginative life of the Jewish people, in its mind and emotions. And that part of the task of description and interpretation is best done by historians of the Jewish people, those who (in the present context) take on the work of relating the social and historical framework of the group to its inner life of feeling, fantasy, and imagination. The question to be asked in this setting is how the distinctive myths and rites of Judaism—its way of shaping life and its way of living—continued to possess the power to form, and to make sense of, an enduring world in diverse and changing contexts. When we consider that Judaism continued in a single, remarkably persistent system for nearly 2,000 years, from the second century to the nineteenth and even the twentieth, we must ask what has so persisted to make sense of the world to the Jews, and of the Jews to their world. That perennial and enduring congruence between myth and circumstance, context and system, surely will enter into our definition of Judaism alongside the elements of process described and choice explained.

My main point is that the defining of the received vision of Judaism is through processes of exegesis, which govern feeling and imagination, make sense of context and situation, and persist over time with remarkable stability. It is the discovery and statement of these rules of process which permit us to speak of Judaism. The work of description is to be done through hermeneutics, history of religions, and history, but these disciplines do not constitute theology; they only define the parameters within which theology is to be done.

First, we must determine what is the text, or the kind of text, upon which theological work is to be done. It seems evident that, in nineteenth- and twentieth-century theological discourse, a wrong choice has been made. For when we ask about the canon upon which modern theologians of Judaism draw, the answer is twofold: modern philosophy of religion, and the Hebrew Scriptures or Written Torah. A few particularly learned theologians cite (episodically to be sure, and not systematically or in context) talmudic sayings too. Proof of this proposition is through a simple mental experiment. When you read the work of nearly all modern voices of Judaism, what books must you know to understand their thought? And what do you *not* need to know? Commonly, you must know Kant and you will do well to know Hegel. You also should know some stories and sayings of the Hebrew Scriptures, the Written Torah, and some tales of the Talmud and midrashim, the Oral Torah. Except for Abraham J. Heschel and Joseph B. Solo-veichik, there is not a single important theologian of the present or past century who cannot be fully and exhaustively understood within those limits, because none draws systematically and routinely upon the other resources of the canon of Judaism. But the entire range of the holy books of Judaism speaks, in particular, through Heschel.

In my judgment Judaism cannot draw for definition solely upon the Written Torah and episodic citations of rabbinic *aggadah*. There are two reasons. First, it has been the whole (Dual) Torah, written and oral, of Moses, our Rabbi, which has defined Judaism through the ages and which must therefore serve today to supply the principal sources of Judaism. Second, this Dual Torah in fact is many, for the canon of Judaism—Torah—has received new documents in every age down to our own.[3] If, therefore, we conclude that the correct sources of Judaic theology are formed of the one whole Torah of Moses, we find ourselves back at the beginning, with the question of canon and hermeneutics of canon—how it is delineated and interpreted.

So the sources of theology of Judaism are the whole and complete canon of Torah. That canon is defined for us by the shelves of books deemed by the consensus of the faithful to be holy and to warrant study in religious circumstances, that is, to be part of Torah. The canon of Torah is sufficiently open so that the words of even living men may be received in faith and recorded in piety. *The processes by which books find their way into that canon define the convictions of Judaism about the character and meaning of revelation.* Furthermore, I am able to point even in our own day to a theologian whose *oeuvres* do conform to the criterion of breadth and rigorous learning as the Judaic canon by which all theology is to be measured and by which most theologians, alas, are found shallow and ignorant.

---

[3]A definition of Judaism that draws principally upon the Written Torah read other than through the perspective of the Oral Torah, its full and exhaustive interpretation, is not Judaism either. That is, so far as there are rules which permit us to speak of Judaism, these rules must be observed. Otherwise we are making things up as we go along and calling our invention Judaism. If we do this, we cannot claim to communicate with other ages and other people in our own age. When there is no shared realm of discourse, past and present, there is that capricious alternation of noise or silence which is, in the life of emotions, the prelude to death and, in the life of the intellect, the symptom of the end of reasoned discourse. Since theology is the work of and for intellectuals pursued through reasoned discourse about, in part, a realm of distinctive and rich emotions and educated feelings, we cannot afford the costs of ignorance and capriciousness.

But the center of Judaism is its way of life. No accurate and careful description of Judaism omits that obvious point. We already have noted that merely describing how Jews now live is not to define the way of life of Judaism. That is a sociological fact. But it is now to be balanced against a theological conviction everywhere affirmed in the history of Judaism since the second century. Judaism expresses its theology through the pattern of deeds performed by the practitioner of Judaism. Judaism is what Judaists are supposed to do. I cannot think of a proposition more widely held in ages past and in our own time than that the theology of Judaism *is* its halakhah, its way of living. If, therefore, we want to describe what Judaism teaches, we have to make sense of what Judaism requires the practitioner of Judaism to practice.[4] But what is the meaning of the practice, and how is that meaning to be uncovered?

Under some circumstances Judaism borders upon orthopraxy (eat *kosher* and think *teraif* [unkosher]—a remarkably vulgar formulation of a theological position) and, under others, upon what Heschel called "religious behaviorism." Religious behaviorists are robots of the law, who will do everything required by the law and think nothing on account of the law. We also find ortho-practitioners—nihilists of the law who do everything by the law and think the law allows thinking anything we like. These corruptions of the faith are revealing. What seems worth noticing in them is that

---

[4]Joseph Dov Soloveichik certainly is to be invoked as a principal exponent of the position outlined here, as in his "Ish hahalakhah," *Talpiyyot* (1944), pp. 651–735, and "The Lonely Man of Faith," *Tradition* 7, no. 2 (1965): 5–67. As Aaron Rothkoff wrote, "The man lives in accordance with the halakhah, he becomes master of himself and the currents of his life . . . he ceases to be a mere creature of a habit. His life becomes sanctified, and God and man are drawn into a community of existence, a 'covenantal community,' which brings God and man together in an intimate, person-to-person relationship. It is only through the observance of the halakhah that man attains this goal to nearness to God" (*Encyclopaedia Judaica*, 15:132–33). It is no criticism to observe that Soloveichik's observations, while profound, thus far are episodic and not systematic. Despite his formidable insights, the work of interpretation of the halakhah as a theological enterprise simply has not yet begun. Nor do I think it can be done by halakhists within the intellectually impoverished resources of their training. They are, to begin with, in no way humanists. Perhaps had Franz Rosenzweig lived he might have done this work, just as he—nearly alone—turned to the *Siddur* as a principal source of theology.

orthopraxy is deemed an acceptable option, while religious behaviorism is rarely recognized, let alone condemned. It is surprising
that there is little effort (Soloveichik here is definitely the exception)
and no wide-ranging, systematic, and *sustained* effort (with no
exception) to state the theology of Judaism principally out of the
sources of the halakhah.[5]

The fact is, however, that so far as Judaism today is a living
religion, it continues its life though halakhah. One authentic
monument to the destruction of European Jewry likely to endure
beyond the present fad is contained in the response literature of the
ghettos and the concentration camps.[6] That is where Judaism is
lived, defined in the crucible of life and death. There is a theology
of Judaism emergent from and triumphant over the "Holocaust,"
but we have yet to hear its message, because we scarcely know how
to listen to Judaism when Judaism speaks idiomatically, as it always

---

[5]Heschel's corpus seems to me probative. I can point in his works to systematic
and profound reflection upon the theology of the whole of the canon of Judaism
except for the halakhic part, that is, that part which, speaking descriptively, all
concur, forms the core. The fact that Heschel lived wholly in accord with the
halakhah is beside the point, just as it is beside the point that another great
theologian of modern Judaism, Martin Buber, did not. What the two have in
common is that through them halakhah did not and does not speak, and, in the
case of Buber, what to begin with is heard from halakhah is simply a negative fact,
the existence of something *against* which theology will find its definition. What we
do have as theology of halakhah in Heschel and Soloveichik is sermonic and not
sustained; it is episodic and not systematic. (Here I shall mercifully leave unnamed
a fair number of Orthodox and Conservative halakhist-theologians.) I say this of
Heschel, however, in full awareness of the unkept promise of his *The Sabbath: Its
Meaning for Modern Man,* which comes as close as any essay in contemporary
theology of Judaism to take up in a systematic and existentially profound way (as
against the intellectual ephemera of sermons) the intellectual premises of halakhah.
There is in the corpus of Heschel no work that draws upon and responds to the
Shulhan Arukh, Maimonides' *Mishneh Torah,* the Talmud as Talmud (not merely
as a storehouse of interesting sayings and stories), or, above all, and the source of
it all, Mishnah and its companion, Tosefta. If it is not in Heschel, then, it is
nowhere else. I cannot point to a single systematic and sustained work of theology
out of the sources of Mishnah and Tosefta, out of the Talmud as a halakhic
monument or any significant part thereof, out of the monuments formed by the
medieval commentaries and codes, down to the present day.

[6]Some of this has been translated into English as *The Holocaust and Halakhah,* by
Irving Rosenbaum (New York, 1976).

has spoken, in accord with the methods and procedures of *its* canon, in obedience to *its* rules, and, above all, in the natural course of the unfolding of *its* consistent and cogent processes of thought and expression. The halakhah endured in the crucible of Warsaw and Lodi when *aggadah* and theology fell dumb.

The coming task of theology in Judaism—the task that will face readers of this collection in their future reflection on the religious life of Judaism—is to define Judaism through the theological study of the neglected canon of the halakhah. To begin with, the canon must be allowed to define its literary frame for theological expression. One of the chief reasons for the persistent failure of the philosophers of halakhah to accomplish what they set out to do is the confusion of their categories. They work through the whole of halakhah on a given subject. They therefore present results entirely divorced from context, on the one side, and from dynamic processes of exegesis, on the other. So they tell us mere facts, a description of what "the halakhah" has to say, without analysis or explanation of meaning. They do not give a clear account of the context in which halakhah framed the message, the setting to which it did so, and the way the message was framed. They therefore tell us about halakhah but do not convey a shred of wisdom or insight into the processes and methods of halakhah relevant to any given age of Judaism, past or present. But the halakhah did not and does not take shape in a timeless world. It is meant to *create* a world beyond time—a different thing. Its genius was to take shape in a very specific, concrete moment yet to transcend that moment and address ages to come as well. We shall not know how that was done if we persist in ignoring the diversity of the context and canon of the halakhah. We have to confront the specificities of its books and their diverse messages and methods, the historicity and religiosity of the halakhah.[7]

---

[7]Just as Heschel could address himself to the issues of religious ontology of the prophets, the rabbis named in Mishnah, Maimonides, Judah Halevi, the Zohar, Hasidic literature, prayerbook, and on down to our own time, so the theologian of halakhah will have to allow each and every document of halakhah to emerge in all its concrete specificity. But where to begin? It is to Mishnah and its tractates and divisions that we look for *one* beginning. But if we do not also look to Scripture and its many codes of law, clearly etched along the lines of the Priestly Code and the

Once the canon is suitably defined in its diversity and specificity, what is it that we wish to know *about* these documents? The first thing is the processes of their unfolding: the processes that have occupied the halakhic thinkers. One significant issue must be how the halakhic process expanded its range to encompass every circumstance confronted by the Jewish people. For Judaism is a world-creating and world-explaining system. The system works through law, and the law functions through processes of argument and discussion. These make intelligible and bring under control of rules all the fresh data of the world which constitute time and change. The system persists because it makes sense of all data and continues to draw new facts into its framework. When it can no longer deal credibly with the new world within this framework, reconcile exegesis of the canon and the newest concerns of the age, the system collapses. Thus, faced by two facts that cannot be brought within the framework of the system of Judaism, Emancipation and modern, political anti-Semitism, Judaism has considerable difficulty. Specifically, it did not succeed in shaping meaningful issues for argument in accord with its established methods. So the theologian will want to reflect upon both how the system works and how it does not work. There is a clear frontier delineated by the end of inner plausibility. There is a border defined by the cessation of self-evidence.[8]

Holiness code on the one side, and the earlier thinking of the Deuteronomica schools on the other, we shall miss yet other beginnings. And I think it is obvious that, for theology as Judaism to be compelling in our own time, it will have to contend with the testimonies of documents standing on the threshold of the canon even now: the Dead Sea Scrolls. In outlining the limits of the halakhic canon, we want to inquire after the processes of thought and the reaching of concrete conclusions of the masters of halakhah, early and late. They who expressed their theology through law and only through law so shaped the social and psychological norms of each age. They surely must define Judaism, not merely the epiphenomena called its "way of life."

[8]Alongside description and interpretation of the processes of exegesis must come a second arena for delineation: the range of choice which the system permits and which it prohibits. One may eat only certain few foods, but the associated problems are rich and engaging. Stated more broadly, the proposition does not change. There is a given way of life defined by the processes of exegesis of the law and through its diverse literature. That way of life has to be described in the

The first two principal tasks of the theologian in Judaism, then, are to define Judaism (vision received) and to correlate Judaism with the life of Jewish people (vision reformed). These tasks are not to be isolated from one another, because the sources of definition of Judaism, the halakhic sources, address themselves to the life of the Jewish people and propose to reshape that life in accord with the paradigm of the holy: *You shall be holy, because I am holy.* In this context, there are two sources for theology in Judaism: first, Torah, whole, unending, a never-to-be-closed canon; and, second, the human experience of the Jewish people raised to the level of Torah through halakhah. Theology in Judaism makes sense of life already lived, but it has to reflect upon the mode of life lived in accord with Torah. What is to be defined and explained is the correlation between the (ideal, normative) human images of the halakhah and the actual shape of life lived in accord with that halakhah. What is this particular kind of humanity that is shaped within the disciplines and critical tensions of the law? What are the larger human meanings to be adduced in interpretation of this particular kind of humanity?

To answer these questions the texts which constitute the sources of theology in Judaism have first to be reread, systematically,

---

context of humanity and of the humanities: what sort of people, society, and culture emerge when life is lived in this way and not in some other. The halakhic literature awaits this kind of mention: description of the life of emotion and of relationship; of the society of home, family, and town; of the choices made and alternatives avoided by the individual and the group. The whole is best framed by the halakhic corpus. Since, moreover, we have access to other great systems of religion expressed through distinctive ways of life—for example, Islam, with its legal literature, its processes of exegesis, and its way of life, as well as Buddhism on the one side and Christianity on the other, both profoundly halakhic constructions at important points in their history—there is a sizable task of comparison to be worked out. So alongside, and cogent with, the description of the processes of Judaism, another task must be done: the comparison of the results, the description of the history of Judaism within the history of religions. Such work may yield that perspective upon which definition must depend. And I need hardly dwell upon the centrality of the work of the historian of the Jews, able to relate the halakhic process to the concrete social and historical circumstances of the Jewish people. For the historian and sociologist of the Jews in the end provide the most interesting evidence about the concrete workings of Judaism.

thoroughly, and, at the outset, historically, one by one. A fresh set of questions has to be devised that will yield four criteria of meaning: (1) the inner issues addressed by the halakhic texts, (2) the human meaning of those issues, when they are interpreted (3) against the particular times and settings in which the texts are framed, and (4) against the continuing social and historical realities of the Jewish people.

To start at the end, we have to know about those ongoing considerations which must be taken into account by all normative statements on behavior and belief, those traits of society and imagination which characterize every context in which Judaism comes to expression and which, therefore, define the other limits of Judaism. Next, we need to discern the particular concerns of a given situation and isolate what is fresh and unanticipated therein. For once we have uncovered the concrete and specific context in which a major conceptual initiative is given shape in halakhah (third criterion), we are able to enter into the human circumstance which will help us to understand the question—the existential problem—dealt with by a given initiative. Finally, it is at that point that we may bring to full articulation the inner issues addressed by the halakhic text. In this way, we are not reducing them to accidents of a given context, but rather confronting them in their ultimate and whole claim to speak in the name of Torah and to talk of holy things, of God and humanity in God's image.

It is principally in the great halakhic texts that the humanistic concerns of theology in Judaism are encapsulated and awaiting discovery. So far as Judaism proposes to express itself through the deeds of the Jewish people and the society which they construct together, we require access to two things. First is philosophical reflection upon the meanings present in common human experience, and second is the language prescribed and expressed within Torah. That common human experience, so far as it is accessible to Torah, is shaped by halakhah—when halakhah is understood for what it is. Let us therefore state what it is and is not.

Halakhah is Judaism's principal expression. But halakhah has been too long set aside since the splendid philosophical-halakhic accomplishment of Maimonides, which was to express the theology of halakhah in its fullness and complexity. If we take halakhah as the

crucial category for the worldview and methods that are defined as
Judaism, then we want to know the range and perspectives of the
vision of the halakhah. What the worldview is that shapes and is
shaped by the ethos of the halakhah, the conceptions of humanity
and of the potentialities of human society—these things await
definition. But, I wish now to suggest, theology is something more
than merely the making explicit of what is implicit and constitutive.

The work of the theologian—as distinct from that of the scholar
of history—must be constructive and creative. Theologians, unlike
scholars, must be granted the freedom as constructive religious
thinkers to propose fresh perspectives on the law, and even
alterations in the worldview and ethos of the law. This freedom, we
know, has been assumed and vigorously exercised by the great
thinkers of the halakhah who understood the deep paradox of the
famous play on words, *herut al halluhot* ("freedom [is] incised upon
the tablets of the law"). If there *is* freedom in discipline, then
theologians cannot be denied the greatest freedom of all: to speak in
fresh and original ways within the halakhic frame, just as they do
within the frame of biblical and aggadic materials. For affirming a
halakhic definition of Judaism is a theological decision, in the rich
sense of the term: the doing of normative and constructive theology.

Theology is not solely the description of theology, the evocation
of worlds past. If it also is not the invocation also of worlds now and
future, it is hardly needed. It is the first task of the theologian to
describe and interpret that world of meaning. But it is the second,
and still more important, task to carry forward the exegesis of the
worldview of Judaism by continuing halakhic reflection upon the
world, thereby shaping a vision of what we are and can be. For in
its way halakhah in the end lays before us a conception of who the
community of Israel is and what the community of Israel can be.
Halakhah speaks of the holiness of that community within the
holiness of God. Its themes and issues then focus upon the way of
life of the community of Israel, to the end that the community may
fulfill its potential as the people of the Lord, the kingdom of priests,
and the holy people. Now when theologians today see the world
within the disciplines of halakhah and the holiness halakhah means
to nurture, their creative and constructive work begins. It is to lay

down statements of continuing norms for a new context. It is to renew the ancient norms through the lessons of a new age. What, after all, do we deal with if not an exploration of human nature and of the divine image impressed within it? And what is at the heart and soul of Judaism if not the inquiry into the image of God in which we are made, therefore into the potential sanctity of us and of the world we make?

We cannot, therefore, concede that the theological work is done for all time in the pages of Maimonides' *Mishneh Torah* or Karo's *Shulhan Arukh*. We insist that the work be done in our own days, when decisions bespeak a vision of who we are and what we can be, of what it means to be in God's image and to live in a community meant to express God's will. The ancient, medieval, and modern rabbis have done more than a work of history and hermeneutics. On the basis of what they are trained to perceive, in every age they forge a new understanding of an unprecedented world. That was what was original for them: Maimonides does not merely quote the ancient sources, though *Mishneh Torah* is a melange of quotations. Through his reflection and arrangement he says something new through something a thousand years old. What we have to learn is that the halakhic process contains the theological process of Judaism. When we understand how that process works, we shall gain access to Judaism. The creation of worlds goes on in world without end. That is what, as Rashi says, it means to be "like God"—to create worlds.

Judaism is a religion about this world and about the human being, who is conceived as being made in God's image and little lower than angels; the community, framed and formed by human beings, is the arena for the working out of God's word and will. Distinctive to Judaism is the intensely practical and practiced law. The word is not abstract. The will is for the here and now. But the word is yet a word, the will is not solely about what I eat but how I understand and feel—and what I am. In the end, we are always mortal, but before we die, we may become something "in our image, according to our likeness," like God. In that painful tension between death and living, between our mortality and the vision of the sacred in ourselves, is the sanctuary of life, the arena for our struggles and anguish. In the pain and the suffering, in the living in the face of the dying, is the sacred. The achievement, the vanquishing and the being vanquished too, are sacred. Holiness is the pathos, holiness, the triumph.

It remains briefly to address two questions: that of usefulness and relevance. At the outset there is a threefold set of tasks of theology in Judaism: (1) to define Judaism, (2) to discover the human situation to which Judaism responds, and (3) to create those modes of advocacy and apologetics which will permit contemporary Jews to gain renewed access to that Judaism subject to definition. This third task may be captured in the question: To whom is such a theological enterprise as I have described going to be useful? To whom, outside of Judaism, are the results of this kind of theology going to be relevant? The two questions are really one, for Jews seeking to define and understand Judaism and scholars of religions asking for definition of religion within the case of Judaism address the authoritative sources with the same fundamental questions: What is this thing—this "Judaism" as we call it in the secular world, this "Torah" as we call it who are believers? How does it work? Believers and scholars part company only at the end. For believers, Jews who also are Judaists, have yet a Judaic question not shared by others: How shall I find my way inside, or, if I am inside, what does it mean to *be* inside? But these questions too prove important to both secular Jews and scholars of religion. The reason, after all, is that the study of all religions must encompass attention to the study of theologies, and no Jew who wishes to respond to the demand of the Torah—to God who calls to us through the Torah—will find a response compelling unless a rich theological substructure is discerned and articulated.

INTRODUCTION: GOD AS PREMISE, PRESENCE, PERSON, AND PERSONALITY

When we propose to describe the theological system to which a piece of well-crafted writing testifies, our task is easy when the writing to begin with discusses in syllogistic logic and within an appropriate program of propositions what we conceive to be theological themes or problems. Hence, it is generally conceded, we may legitimately translate the topically theological writings of Paul, Augustine, or Luther into the systematic and coherent theologies of those three figures, finding order and structure in materials of a cogent theological character. But what about a literature—such as the literature of the oral part of the Torah that defines Judaism—that to begin with does not set forth theological propositions in philosophical form, even while using profoundly religious language for religious purposes? Surely that literature testifies to an orderly structure or system of thought, for the alternative is to impute to the contents of those writings the status of mere episodic and unsystematic observations about this and that. True, profound expressions of piety may exhibit the traits of intellectual chaos and disorder, and holy simplicity may mask confusion. But such a description of the rabbinic literature of late antiquity, which I call the canon of the Judaism of the Dual Torah, defies the most definitive and indicative traits of the writings.

These traits are order, system, cogency, coherence, proportion, and fine and well-crafted thought. As I shall explain presently, the Mishnah, with which the writing down of the Oral Torah begins, is a profoundly philosophical statement; the two Talmuds presuppose the harmony and unity of the conceptions of the Mishnah and their own conceptions; the various Midrash-compilations make statements that exhibit intellectual integrity; they show the marks not of confusion and contradiction, but of variety and richness, and they assuredly do not merely compile ad hoc and episodic observations. *Lamentations Rabbah*, *Ruth Rabbah*, *Esther Rabbah*, and *Song of Songs Rabbah* each say one thing in a great many ways, so, by their own character, these writings point toward some sort of logic and order and structure that find attestation in the writings themselves. And when we seek to articulate the principles of order and structure as these pertain to the fundamental characteristics of God, the Torah, and Israel, we set forth the theology of the canon of the Judaism of the Dual Torah.

This collection undertakes to describe the three principal parts of the theological system that gives sense, structure, and cogency to the Oral Torah's fundamental convictions, to set them forth in a schematic and exemplary way to be sure that the theology makes the literature coherent in sense and in meaning. The canonical writings, appealing to God's revelation to Moses at Sinai, everywhere calling upon God and spelling out what God wants of Israel in quest of God and God's service, form one of the great religious writings of humanity. These writings yield theology in addition to religion, and here I mean for us to see them not merely as a vast and confusing mass of half-coherent thoughts, for us to test the perception of order amid the appearance of chaos, such as these writings create.

To begin with, we have to justify the theological inquiry into literature that self-evidently does not conform to the conventions of theological discourse to which Western civilization in its Greco-Roman heritage and Christian (and, as a matter of fact, Muslim) civilization in its philosophical formulation have accustomed us. The Muslim and Christian theological heritage, formulated within the conventions of philosophical argument, joined by a much smaller Judaic theological corpus to be sure, does not allow us to

read as a theological statement a single canonical writing of the
Judaism of the Dual Torah of late antiquity. Therefore if the literary
canons of Western theology are to govern, then the literature of
Judaism in its formative age can present no theological order and
system at all.

But that proposition on the face of it hardly proves compelling.
For it is difficult for us to imagine a mental universe so lacking in
structure, form, and order as to permit everything and its opposite
to be said about God, to imagine a God so confused and self-
contradictory as to yield a revelation lacking all cogency and being
truly unintelligible.[1] The very premises of all theology—that there is
structure, composition, and proportion in God's mind, which is
intelligible to us through revelation properly construed—a priori
render improbable such a hypothesis. If, after all, we really cannot
speak intelligibly about God, the Torah, holy Israel, and what God
wants of us, then why write all those books to begin with?

The character of the literature, its rather hermetic modes of
discourse, arcane language of thought, insistence upon speaking

---

[1]As a matter of fact, the great Zoroastrian theologians of the ninth century
criticized Judaism (and other religions) on just this point; see my "Zoroastrian
Critique of Judaism," reprinted in my *History of the Jews in Babylonia* (Leiden: E. J.
Brill, 1969) 4:403–423. But not a single Judaic thinker, either philosopher or
theologian, either in the Islamic philosophical tradition or in the Western
theological and philosophical tradition, has ever entertained the proposition that
the God who gave the Torah is confused and arbitrary. And why should anyone
have thought so, when, after all, the entire dynamic of Judaic thought embodied
within the great halakhic tradition from the Yerushalmi and Bavli forward has
aimed at the systematization, harmonization, and ordering of confusing, but never
confused, facts of the Torah. There is, therefore, no possibility of finding in the
Judaism of the Dual Torah the slightest hint of an unsystematic system, an
atheological corpus of thought. True, a fixed truth of the theological system
known as *die Wissenschaft des Judenthums* has maintained that "Judaism has no
theology," but that system knew precisely what it meant by *Judaism,* even while
never explaining what it might mean by the *theology* that that Judaism did not have.
But that is a problem of description, analysis, and interpretation for those who take
an interest in the system of thought that underpins "Jewish scholarship" and
Reform Judaism in particular, that is, specialists in the history of ideas in the
nineteenth century, and of the nineteenth century in the twentieth century. These
are not statements of fact that must be taken into account in describing, analyzing,
and interpreting documents of the Judaism of the Dual Torah.

only about detail and rarely about the main point—these traits stand in the way of the description of theology because of their very unsyllogistic character. And yet, if we consider not the received modes of discourse of theology in our civilization but rather the problem and topic of theology—systematic and orderly thinking about God, about how we know God, and about the definition of this "we," the holy community of the faithful, that come into being through the medium of revelation—we can hardly find a more substantial or suitable corpus of writing for theological analysis than the literature of the Judaism of the Dual Torah.

For while theology may comprise well crafted and cogently structured propositions about fundamental questions of God and revelation, the social entity that realizes that revelation, the attitudes and deeds that God, through revelation, requires of humanity, there is another way entirely. Theology can deliver its message not only through thought and expression that yield belief, but also through sentiment and emotion, heart as well as mind; it can be conviction as much as position, and conviction also is orderly and proportioned, compelling of mind and intellect by reason of right attitude rather than right proposition or position. Theology may set forth a system of thought in syllogistic arguments concerning the normative truths of the worldview, social entity, and way of life of a religious system but do so in other than dynamic and compelling argument, and theologians may speak truth about God through other than the statements made by language and in conformity with the syntax of reasoned thought.

Theology may also be expressed in tactile ways; it may utilize a vocabulary not of proposition but of opaque symbol (through visual or verbal media), and may thereby affect attitude and emotion, speak its truth through other media than philosophy and proposition. From the time of Martin Buber's *Two Types of Faith,* nearly four decades ago, people have understood that this other type of theology, the one that lives in attitude and sentiment and that evokes and demands trust, may coexist, or even compete, with the philosophical type to whose discourse we are accustomed. How then do we meet God in the pages of the Oral Torah?

The Oral Torah portrays God in four ways: as premise, presence, person, and personality. A definitive statement of the proposition that God appears to humanity in diverse forms opens the door to this essay. We begin with the following:

Pesiqta deRab Kahana XII:XXV

Another interpretation of *I am the Lord your God [who brought you out of the land of Egypt]*(Exodus 20:2):

Said R. Hinena bar Papa, "The Holy One, blessed be he, had made his appearance to them with a stern face, with a neutral face, with a friendly face, with a happy face.

"with a stern face: in Scripture. When a man teaches his son Torah, he has to teach him in a spirit of awe.

"with a neutral face: in Mishnah.

"with a friendly face: in Talmud.

"with a happy face: in lore.

"Said to them the Holy One, blessed be he, 'Even though you may see all of these diverse faces of mine, nonetheless: *I am the Lord your God who brought you out of the land of Egypt* (Exodus 20:2)."

So far we deal with attitudes. As to the iconic representation of God, the following is explicit:

Said R. Levi, "The Holy One, blessed be he, had appeared to them like an icon that has faces in all directions, so that if a thousand people look at it, it appears to look at them as well.

"So too when the Holy One, blessed be he, when he was speaking, each and every Israelite would say, 'With me in particular the Word speaks.'

"What is written here is not, I am the Lord, your [plural] God, but rather, *I am the Lord your [singular] God who brought you out of the land of Egypt* (Exodus 20:2)."

That God may show diverse faces to various people is now established. The reason for God's variety is made explicit. People differ, and God, in the image of whom all mortals are made, must therefore sustain diverse images—all of them formed in the model of human beings:

Said R. Yose bar Hanina, "And it was in accord with the capacity of each one of them to listen and understand what the Word spoke with him.

"And do not be surprised at this matter, for when the mana came down to Israel, each and every one would find its taste appropriate to his capacity, infants in accord with their capacity, young people in accord with their capacity, old people in accord with their capacity.

"infants in accord with their capacity: just as an infant sucks from the tit of his mother, so was its flavor, as it is said, *Its taste was like the taste of rich cream* (Numbers 11:8).

"young people in accord with their capacity: as it is said, *My bread also which I gave you, bread and oil and honey* (Ezekiel 16:19).

"old people in accord with their capacity: as it is said *the taste of it was like wafers made with honey* (Exodus 16:31).

"Now if in the case of mana, each and every one would find its taste appropriate to his capacity, so in the matter of the Word, each and every one understood in accord with capacity.

"Said David, *The voice of the Lord is [in accord with one's] in strength* (Psalms 29:4).

"What is written is not, *in accord with his strength in particular,* but rather, *in accord with one's strength,* meaning, in accord with the capacity of each and every one.

"Said to them the Holy One, blessed be He, 'It is not in accord with the fact that you hear a great many voices, but you should know that it is I who [speaks to all of you individually]: *I am the Lord your God who brought you out of the land of Egypt* (Exodus 20:2).' "

The individuality and particularity of God rest upon the diversity of humanity. But, it must follow that the model of humanity—"in our image"—dictates how we are to envisage the face of God. That is the starting point of our inquiry. The Torah defines what we know about God, but it also tells us that we find God in the face of the other: "in our image," means everyone is in God's image, so if we want to know God, we had best look closely into the face of all humanity, one by one, one by one.

In the Oral Torah we find God portrayed in the earlier writings as (1) premise and (2) presence, then in later writings as (3) person as well, and finally, in the last phase of the formation of the Oral Torah, the Talmud of Babylonia, as (4) personality. Let us consider these four dimensions of God, the measure by which we grasp the character of divinity in the Judaism under study. These dimensions are concrete and specific; we can readily determine where, when, and how we may take the measure dictated by each of them.

1. By God as premise, I refer to passages in which an authorship reaches a particular decision because that authorship believes God created the world and has revealed the Torah to Israel. We therefore know that God forms the premise of a passage because the proposition of that passage appeals to God as premise of all being, such as author and authority of the Torah. That conviction of the givenness of this God defines the premise of all Judaisms before our own times. There is nothing surprising in it. But a particular indicator, in so general a fact, derives from the cases in which for specific reasons, in particular cases, sages invoke God as foundation and premise of the world. When do they decide a case or reach a decision because they appeal to God as premise, and when do they not do so? But as we shall see in Chapter 2, this conception is much more subtle, since the entire foundation of the Mishnah rests upon the conception of the unity of God. The purpose of the Mishnah is to show how, in the here and now of the social and natural world, we see what it means that God is one.

2. God as presence stands for yet another consideration: God is referred to as part of a situation in the here and now. When an authorship—of the Mishnah, for example—speaks of an ox goring another ox, it does not appeal to God to reach a decision for them and does not suggest that God has witnessed the event and plans to intervene. However, when the authorship speaks of a wife's being accused of unfaithfulness to her husband, that authorship expects that God will intervene in a particular case, in the required ordeal, and thus will declare the decision for the case. In the former instance, God is assuredly a premise of discourse, having revealed in the Torah the rule governing a goring ox. In the latter, God is not only premise but very present in the discourse and the decision making. God furthermore constitutes a person in certain settings but not in others.

3. One may readily envisage God either as premise or as presence without invoking a notion of the particular traits or personality of God. There is a setting, however, in which God is held always to know and pay attention to specific cases. It involves God as a "You," that is, as a presence. For example, all discourse in the Mishnah that concerns liturgy (obviously not only in that document) understands that God also hears prayer and hence is not

only a presence but a person, a You, responding to what is said, requiring certain attitudes and rejecting others. In a later document, by contrast, God is not only present but a participant, if only implicitly, when the Torah is studied among disciples of sages. Here too we find an interesting indicator of how God is portrayed in one situation as a premise, in a second as a presence, and in a third as a person. In cases in which God is portrayed as a person, however, there are rules and regulations to which God adheres. These permit us to imagine that God is present, without wondering what particular response God may make to a specific situation, such as within the liturgy. We do not have to wonder, because the rules tell us. Accordingly, while God is a liturgical "You," God as person still is not represented in full particularity, reaching a decision on a specific case in accord with traits of mind or heart or soul that yield out of a unique personality, a concrete decision or feeling or action.

4. God emerges as a vivid and highly distinctive personality, actor, conversation partner, hero. In references to God as a personality, God is given corporeal traits. God looks like God in particular, just as each person exhibits distinctive physical traits. Furthermore, in matters of heart and mind and spirit, well-limned individual traits of both personality and action endow God with that particularity that identifies every individual human being. When God is given attitudes but no active role in discourse, referred to but not invoked as part of a statement, God serves as person. When God participates as a hero and protagonist in a narrative, God gains traits of personality and emerges as God like humanity: God incarnate.

The Hebrew Scriptures had long ago portrayed God in richly personal terms: God wants, cares, demands, regrets, says and does—just like human beings. In the Written Torah God is not merely a collection of abstract theological attributes and thus rules for governance of reality, nor a mere person to be revered and feared. God is a specific, highly particular personality, whom people can know, envision, engage, persuade, impress. Sages painted this portrait of a personality through narratives, telling stories in which God figures like incarnate heroes. When therefore the authorships of documents of the oral half of the Dual Torah began to represent

God as personality, they reentered that realm of discourse about God that Scripture had originally laid out. It was not inevitable that some sages, represented by the authorship of the Bavli, should have done so. True, that legacy of Scripture's God as actor and personality constituted for the creators of the Judaism of the Dual Torah an available treasury of established facts about God—hence God incarnate. But within the Scripture the sages picked and chose, and they did so with regard to God as well. At some points in the unfolding corpus, without regard to the entire range of available facts of Scripture, God was represented only as implicit premise, in others, as presence and source of action, in still others as person. So the repertoire of Scripture tells us solely what might have been. It was only at the end, in the Bavli, that we reach the portrayal, much as in Scripture and on the strength of Scripture's facts, of God as personality, with that same passionate love for Israel with which Scripture's authorships had defined God in the received, Written Torah.

People who think that we may know God entirely on our own, discovering God for the first time when we get up in the morning, treat the knowledge of God as personal and private. But, as this brief account of what we are going to find out about God in the Oral Torah already has made clear, in Judaism we do not discover God on our own, nor is the knowledge of God accessible mainly through our individual experience. Though all Judaic religious experience addresses the human being in the here and now, because we have the Torah as the record of what God says to us, we always know God not by ourselves, but through the Torah, that is, by means of Israel's access to the record of God's revelation. The Torah comes to us all, in community. In community, we learn what God is and does and wants of us. Our knowledge of God is traditional, in that it is handed down from generation to generation, as much as it is immediate; it is public and communal as much as it is personal and individual; *we* not only I, know God.

We pray to God always as *we,* even when we are by ourselves, because our quest for God is not private, unprecedented, and subjective. God, as an act of surpassing love and grace, gave the Torah to Israel, the holy people. So our meeting with God is public. It comes from generation to generation, always surprising yet always reliable. And it is objective: God calls, we respond, and the act of faith attests to the invitation to faith. Ours is not a leap of faith. Ours is a response to a God whose call provokes us to wonder. That is why, in the theology of Judaism, the right question about God is not whether or not God exists, nor even what God is like, but rather what God wants of me, and how within holy Israel, the Jewish people, I can make myself into what the Torah says I am, which is in God's image and after God's likeness. That is why our quest for God begins—though it does not end—in the Torah, written and oral alike, and any account, such as this one, of what the theology of Judaism teaches about God must begin in that same place.

Then who is God, who calls, to whom we respond? In Judaism God comes to us in terms we human beings can grasp, even though what we say about God—creator of heaven and earth—refers to God beyond time, beyond space, beyond all conceiving. The gift of the Torah is to tell us that God is described "in the image, after the likeness" of humanity. The conception of humanity in the image of God then portrays God as a human being, a sublime idea that will not for one minute have surprised the authors of a variety of Judaic documents, beginning with the compilers of the Pentateuch. Some speaking explicitly, others in subtle allusions, prophets and apocalyptic writers, exegetes and sages, mystics and legists, all maintained that notion. No single genre of writing—law, prophecy, wisdom, history—exercised a monopoly over the presentation of God as a man. The authorities who made decisions about canonical writings, it is commonly held, took the view that the Song of Songs spoke of God's love for Israel, and, it follows, the view that God took the form of a young man, stated in *Pesiqta deRab Kahana,* would have proved entirely acceptable in those circles that received the Song in their canon of Scripture.

The canon of the Judaism that emerged from ancient times and governed to our own day, "the Torah," was in two parts. One was the Hebrew Scriptures of ancient Israel ("the Old Testament"), called in this Judaism the Written Torah, and the other was a set of writings later accorded the status of Torah as well and assigned origin at Sinai through a process of oral formulation and transmission, hence the Oral Torah.

The first and most important of those writings that came to comprise the Oral Torah was the Mishnah, ca. 200. That document carried in its wake two sustained amplifications and extensions called *talmuds,* the one produced in the Land of Israel, hence the Talmud of the Land of Israel, ca. 400, the other in Babylonia, in the Iranian Empire, hence the Talmud of Babylonia, ca. 600.

The Written Torah also served analogously to define a framework for (formally) continuous discourse and so received a variety of sustained amplifications, called Midrash-compilations. These were in three sets, corresponding to the Mishnah, the Talmud of the Land of Israel, and the Talmud of Babylonia. In this anthology we deal only with the Oral Torah.

The first Midrash-compilation, within the orbit of the Mishnah, ca. 200–300, addressed the books of Exodus, Leviticus, Numbers, and Deuteronomy: *Mekhilta,* attributed to R. Ishmael, for Exodus, *Sifra* for Leviticus, one *Sifré* for Numbers, another *Sifré* for Deuteronomy. The Mishnah set forth in the form of a law code a highly philosophical account of the world ("worldview"), a pattern for everyday and material activities and relationships ("way of life"), and a definition of the social entity ("nation," "people," "us" as against "outsiders," "Israel") that realized that way of life and explained it by appeal to that worldview. Then the successor documents, closed roughly two centuries later, addressed the Mishnah's system and recast its categories into a connected but also quite revised one.

Why call them *successors?* Because, in form, the writings of the late fourth and fifth centuries were organized and presented as commentaries on a received text, the Talmud on Mishnah, and the Midrash-compilations on the Scripture. So the later authorships insisted, in their own behalf, that they (merely) explained and amplified the received Torah. When these documents attached themselves to the Mishnah and to the Hebrew Scriptures, they gave literary form to the theory that the one stood for the Oral and the other for the Written Torah that God gave to Moses at Mount Sinai.

Specifically, the Talmud of the Land of Israel, formed around thirty-nine of the Mishnah's sixty-two tractates, and *Genesis Rabbah* and *Leviticus Rabbah* (joined by *Pesiqta deRab Kahana*) addressed the first and third books of Moses, respectively, along with some other documents. The very act of choosing only some of the Mishnah's tractates and ignoring others, of course, represents an act of taste and judgment—hence system-building through tacit statement made by silence. But, as a matter of fact, much of the Talmud as well as of the principal Midrash-compilations do amplify and augment the base documents to which they are attached.[2] In choosing some passages and neglecting others, and, more to the point, in working out their own questions and answers in addition to those of the Mishnah, the authorships[3] attest to a system that did more than merely extend and recast the categorical structure of the system for which the Mishnah stands. They took over the way of life, worldview, and social entity defined in the Mishnah's system. And while they rather systematically amplified details, framed a program of exegesis around the requirements of clerks engaged in enforcing the rules of the Mishnah, they built their own system.

Now to the story before us. In the oral part of the Torah as much as in the written part, God, who created the world and gave the Torah to Moses, encounters Israel in a vivid and personal way. But while some of the documents of the Oral Torah portray God only as a premise, presence, and person, others represent God as a personality, specifically like a human being with whom people may

---

[2]My estimate for the Talmud of the Land of Israel, in the tractates I probed, is that, in volume, as much as 90 percent of the Talmud serves to amplify passages of the Mishnah, and not much more than 10 percent contains intellectual initiatives that are fundamentally fresh and unrelated to anything in the Mishnah passage under discussion. (See my *Talmud of the Land of Israel. XXXV. Introduction: Taxonomy* (Chicago: The University of Chicago Press, 1983). Then my *Judaism in Society: The Evidence of the Yerushalmi: Toward the Natural History of a Religion* (Chicago, 1983) aims to show that even the passages that (merely) clarify words or phrases of the Mishnah in fact set forth a considerable, autonomous program of their own; cf. especially pages 73–112. But what is clearly distinct from the Mishnah is set forth on pages 113–254.

[3]This term is meant to take account of the collective and social character of much of the literary enterprise. Not a single authoritative book of Judaism in late antiquity bears the name of an identified author, and the literary traits of not a single piece of writing may securely be imputed to a private person. The means for gaining acceptance was anonymity, and the medium of authority lay in recapitulating collective conventions of rhetoric and logic, not to mention proposition. To speak of "authors" in this context is confusing, and hence the resort to the word at hand.

identify and whom they may know, love, and emulate. The categories of premise, presence, and person hardly require much explanation. As premise, God forms (in philosophical terms) the ground of being; that is how God plays a principal part in the Mishnah. Otherwise uncharacterized, God may form a presence and be present in all things. As a person, again without further amplification, God is a "You," for example, to whom people address prayers. When portrayed as a personality, however, God is represented in an incarnate way, not merely by appeal to anthropomorphic metaphors, but by allusions to God's corporeal form, traits of attitude and emotion like those of human beings, capacity to do the sorts of things mortals do in the ways in which they do them. In all of these ways, the incarnation of God is accomplished as in treating God as a personality.

In writings redacted in the earlier stages in the formation of the Judaism of the Dual Torah, beginning with the Mishnah, therefore, God does not make an appearance as a vital personality, with whom human personalities transact affairs. Other documents, in particular in the later stages in the unfolding of that canonical system, by contrast, represent God in quite personal terms. These, as was already suggested, are three: outer traits, inner characteristics, and capacity for concrete action done as human beings carry out their wishes.

What we shall see, therefore, is that the Babylonian Talmud, which is the final statement of the formative period of the Judaism of the Dual Torah, gives us our abiding and compelling account of God. That Talmud represents God in the flesh in the analogy of the human person. And yet, I hasten to add, in that portrayal of the character of divinity, God always remained God. The insistent comparison of God with humanity "in our image and likeness" comes to its conclusion in one sentence that draws humanity upward and does not bring God downward. For despite its treatment of the sage as a holy man, the Bavli's characterization of God never confused God with a sage or a sage with God. Quite to the contrary, the point and purpose of that characterization reaches its climax in a story that in powerful language demands that in the encounter with the sage of all sages God be left to be God: "Silence, for that is how I have decided matters."

How do our sages of blessed memory portray what it means to

know God "in our image, after our likeness"? Here is the answer, in a stunning account.

Genesis Rabbah VIII:X

Said R. Hoshaiah, "When the Holy One, blessed be he, came to create the first man, the ministering angels mistook him [for God, since man was in God's image,] and wanted to say before him, 'Holy, [holy, holy is the Lord of hosts].'

"To what may the matter be compared? To the case of a king and a governor who were set in a chariot, and the provincials wanted to greet the king, 'Sovereign!' But they did not know which one of them was which. What did the king do? He turned the governor out and put him away from the chariot, so that people would know who was king.

"So too when the Holy One, blessed be he, created the first man, the angels mistook him [for God]. What did the Holy One, blessed be he, do? He put him to sleep, so everyone knew that he was a mere man.

"That is in line with the following verse of Scripture: 'Cease you from man, in whose nostrils is a breath, for how little is he to be accounted' (Isaiah 2:22)."

Accordingly, our sages saw God enthroned, riding horses or chariots. Not only so, but given the exegesis of the Song of Songs as a love song between God and Israel, on which basis that book found its way into the canon of Judaism, we must suppose many accepted the invitation. But even such a stunning conception of ourselves like God and God like ourselves does not exhaust the power of the human imagination. Quite to the contrary, it is only in page after page of *Song of Songs Rabbah* that the full and complete statement of who God is to us, and what we are to God, is made. There the Song of Songs is read as a passionate love song, in which Israel responds to God's insistent love.

Reading the Song of Songs as a metaphor for God's and Israel's intense love for one another, our sages find in the scriptural poem the meanings of the *is* in response to the messages of the *as-if*; in these pages we see with great clarity the outer limits of their labor.

"The Song of Songs":
the best of songs, the most excellent of songs, the finest of songs.

"Let us recite songs and praise the One who has made us a remnant for the world: 'The Lord alone shall lead him [Simon: in solitude]'(Deuteronomy 32:12)."

R. Yohanan in the name of R. Aha in the name of R. Simeon b. Abba: "Let us recite songs and praise for the One who will one day cause the Holy Spirit to come to rest upon us.

"Let us say before him many songs."

In all other songs, either He praises them, or they praise him.

In the Song of Moses, they praise him, saying, "This is my God and I will glorify him" (Exodus 15:2).

In the Song of Moses, he praises them: "He made him ride on the high places of the earth" (Deuteronomy 32:13).

Here, [in Song of Songs] they praise him and he praises them.

He praises them: "Behold, you are beautiful, my love; behold, you are beautiful; your eyes are doves."

They praise him: "Behold, you are beautiful, my beloved, truly lovely" (Song of Songs 1:15–16).

For here—if we ask what is the *is* of which the *as-if* forms the metaphor—the *is* is the love of man for woman and woman for man, and the *as-if* is the love of God for Israel and Israel for God. So real and concrete is that poetry, that understanding its implicit meanings, identifying its hidden messages as an account of the lovers, God and Israel, and the urgency of their love for one another—these represent a triumph of the *as-if* mentality over the mentality of the merely-*is*. But the poem the Song of Songs in the hands of our sages of blessed memory is the metaphor, and the reality is the tangible and physical love of Israel for God and of God for Israel: the urgent, never fully satisfied desire. Given the character of the Song of Songs, our sages' power to grasp its wholly-other meanings and plausibly to state them attests to the full givenness of their affirmations of God and Israel as the principal figures in contention—as the lover and the beloved must always contend—in this world. We move a long way from the cool and well-crafted affirmations of one God, pinnacle of creation, to whom all life comes and from whom all life flows, to the hot and impetuous and spontaneous explosions of God's love for Israel and Israel's love for God that punctuate the final chapter in the shaping of the Oral Torah's statement in the formative age. That is the tale I mean to portray in these selections.

It remains to explain the organization of this book as it lays out the sources of the Judaism of the Dual Torah. In line with my description of the parts of the Oral Torah, I deal with the canonical writings in groups: in Part I, the Mishnah and its close companions, the Tosefta and tractate *Avot;* then in the same context the secondary and transitional writings, *Sifra* and the two *Sifrés* (ca. 100–300 C.E.). In Part II, I take up the first of the two Talmuds, the Yerushalmi, and its close friends, *Genesis Rabbah* and *Leviticus Rabbah* with *Pesiqta deRab Kahana* (ca. 300–500 C.E.). In Part III, we consider the final statement, the second of the two Talmuds, the Bavli (ca. 500–700 C.E.). A brief introduction to the documents subject to review here is now in order.

The first of these groups of writings begins with the Mishnah, a philosophical law book brought to closure at ca. C.E. 200 and later on called the first statement of the Oral Torah. In its wake, the Mishnah drew tractate *Avot,* ca. C.E. 250, a statement concluded a generation after the Mishnah on the standing of the authorities of the Mishnah; Tosefta, ca. C.E. 300, a compilation of various kinds of supplements to the statements in the Mishnah; and two systematic exegeses of books of the Written Torah, *Sifra* to Leviticus, *Sifré* to Numbers, and another *Sifré* to Deuteronomy, of indeterminate date but possibly concluded by C.E. 300.

These books form one stage in the unfolding of the Judaism of the Dual Torah, which stressed issues of sanctification of the life of Israel, the people, in the aftermath of the destruction of the Temple of Jerusalem in C.E. 70; in this stage, it was commonly held, Israel's sanctification came to full realization in the bloody rites of sacrifice to God on high. I call this system a Judaism without Christianity, because the urgent issues in the documents of this phase address questions not pertinent to the Christian *défi* of Israel at all. The authorities cited in *Sifra* and the two *Sifrés* are pretty much the same as those in the Mishnah and Tosefta. Since the three documents cite both the Mishnah and the Tosefta verbatim, they presumably came to closure some time after the other documents. But they remain well within the circle of inquiry and exegesis drawn by the authorship of the Mishnah, and if we impute a date of ca. 300 we are not likely to be far off the mark. But that is only a guess. The more substantial reason for treating *Sifra* and the two *Sifrés* within the framework of the Mishnah is their authorships' recurrent concern with demonstrating that teachings of the Mishnah rest upon the authority of the Written Torah, Scripture, and not upon unfettered reason.

The second set of the same writings begins with the Talmud of the Land of Israel, or Yerushalmi, generally supposed to have come to a conclusion at ca. C.E. 400; *Genesis Rabbah,* assigned to about the next half century; *Leviticus Rabbah,* ca. C.E. 450; *Pesiqta deRab Kahana,* ca. C.E. 450–500; and, finally, the Talmud of Babylonia or Bavli, assigned to the late sixth or early seventh century, ca. C.E. 600. The two Talmuds systematically interpret passages of the Mishnah, and the other documents do the same for books of the Written Torah. Some other treatments of biblical books important in synagogue liturgy, particularly *Lamentations Rabbati, Esther Rabbah,* and the like are also supposed to have reached closure at this time. This second set of writings introduces, alongside the paramount issue of Israel's sanctification, the matter of Israel's salvation, with doctrines of history, on the one side, and the Messiah, on the other, given prominence in the larger systemic statement. The Judaic system of the Dual Torah, expressed in its main outlines in the Yerushalmi and associated compilations of biblical exegeses concerning Genesis, Leviticus, and some other scriptural books, culminated in the Bavli. That second Talmud emerged as the authoritative document of the Judaism of the Dual Torah from then to now. At the beginning of Parts I and II I shall expand on these matters.

In the analysis that follows, we shall organize our inquiry in accord with the three types of materials that form cogent statements within the larger canon of the Judaism of the Dual Torah. These cogent statements are, first, those built around the exegesis of the Oral Torah, the Mishnah; second, those that serve to amplify the Written Torah, Scripture; and, finally, those that find cogency in the life and teaching of a given sage or group of sages. Thus there were three modes of organizing large-scale discourse in the Judaism of the Dual Torah. One was to make use of books or verses or themes of Scripture. A second was to compose a systematic commentary and amplification that followed the order of the Mishnah. This was the way, for example, of those who created the Talmud of the Land of Israel a century or so before. A third was to organize stories about and sayings of sages. These were framed around twin biographical principles: either as strings of stories about great sages of the past or as collections of sayings and comments drawn together solely because the same name stands behind the sayings.

The authorship of the Bavli for its part took up materials, in various stages of completion, pertinent to the Mishnah or to the principles of laws that the Mishnah had originally brought to articulation. Second, they had in hand received materials, again in various conditions, pertinent to the Scripture, both as the Scripture related to the Mishnah and also as it laid forth its own narratives. Finally, they collected and arranged sayings of and stories about sages. But this third principle of organizing discourse took a subordinate position behind the other two. The framers of the Bavli organized it around the Mishnah. Second, they adapted and included vast tracts of antecedent materials organized as scriptural commentary and inserted them whole and complete, not at all in response to the Mishnah's program. Finally, while making provision for compositions built upon biographical principles, preserving both strings of sayings from a given master (and often a given tradent of a given master) and tales about authorities of the preceding half millennium, they did nothing new.

That is to say, the ultimate authorships of the canonical documents never created a sizable order of redactional compositions that focused upon given authorities, even though sufficient materials lay at hand for doing so. God's will reached Israel through Scripture, Mishnah, sage—and by the equal evidence and testimony of each. That is the premise of the Judaism of the entire rabbinic canon, of each of the stories that appeal to a verse of Scripture, a phrase or sentence of the Mishnah, or a teaching or action of a sage. Recognizing the three components of the single canon, the Written Torah, the Oral Torah, and the sage as the living Torah, leads us deep into the investigation at hand, to which we now turn.

PART I

The Mishnah's God
of the Philosophers

1

God in Principle

P hilosophy is the queen of sciences, since all other disciplines of learning emerged from it. But it is also the most abstract and difficult to follow, and once we grasp how the Torah was set forth in philosophical modes of thought, everything else will prove rather easy by comparison. The Mishnah, which states its share of the Torah in a philosophical way, is the foundation document of the Oral Torah, and we naturally expect that it will state what we know about God in an intellectually rigorous and demanding way. And we are not going to be disappointed.

In the Mishnah, as in all other writings of Judaism, God is present not merely in details, when actually mentioned, but at the foundations. To characterize the encounter with God, whether intellectual or concrete and everyday, we must therefore pay attention not only to passages that speak of God in some explicit way, but even more to the fundamental givens on which all particular doctrines or stories of a document depend. What that fact means in the case of the Mishnah is simple. That great philosophical law code demonstrates over and over again that all things are one, complex things yield uniform and similar components, and, rightly understood, there is a hierarchy of being, to be discovered through the proper classification of all things. What this means is that, for the philosophers who wrote the Mishnah, the most important thing they wished to demonstrate about God is that God is one. And this they proposed to prove by showing, in a vast array of everyday circumstances, (1) the fundamental order and unity of all things, all being, and (2) the unity of all things in an ascending order to God. So all things, through their unity and order to one thing, and all being derive from One God.

In the Mishnah, many things are placed into sequence and

order—"hierarchized"—and the order of all things is shown to have a purpose, so that the order, or hierarchization, is purposive, or "teleological." The Mishnah time and again demonstrates two contrary propositions: (1) many things join together by their nature into one thing, and (2) one thing yields many things. These propositions of course complement each other, because, in forming matched opposites, the two set forth an ontological judgment. It is that all things not only are orderly, but, in their deepest traits of being, so are ordered that many things fall into one classification, and one thing may hold together many things of a single classification. For this philosophy, then, rationality consists in the hierarchy of the order of things, a rationality tested and proved, time and again, by the possibility always of effecting the hierarchical classification of all things. The proposition that is the Mishnah's, then, is a theory of the right ordering of each thing in its classification (or taxon), all the categories (or taxa) in correct sequence, from least to greatest. And showing that all things can be ordered, and that all orders can be set into relationship with one another, we transform the ontological message into its components of proposition, argument, and demonstration.

The Mishnah's authorship's sustained effort therefore is to demonstrate how many classes of things—actions, relationships, circumstances, persons, places—really form one class. This work of classification then explores the potentialities of chaos, but that exploration is a journey to explicit order. It is classification transformed from the *how* of intellection to the *why* and the *what for* and, above all, the *what does it all mean* of philosophical conviction. The goal is to show, through the very qualities of the natural and social world, that all things point to the plan and purpose of the one God, who so ordered creation as to reveal the divine plan for a well-ordered world: everything in its proper place, each with its rightful name, all things in the order in which, in six days, they were made.

Recognition that one thing may fall into several categories and many things into a single one comes to expression for the authorship of the Mishnah in a simple way. The authorship shows over and over again that diversity in species or diversification in actions follows orderly lines, thus confirming the claim that there is that single point from which many lines come forth. Carried out in proper order, (1) the many form one thing, (2) one thing yields many, the demonstration then leaves no doubt as to the truth of the matter.

The upshot may be stated very simply. The species point to the genus, the classes to one class, and all classes of things, or taxa, properly hierarchized then rise to the top of the structure and the system, forming one taxon. So all things ascend to and reach one thing. All that remains is for the philosopher to define that one thing: God. But that is a step that the philosophers of the Mishnah did not take, at least not in an articulated way. I assume that the reason was that they did not think they had to make such an obvious point. But I think there is a further and altogether different reason. It is because they were in fact philosophers who were not theologians at all. The document they produced pursues issues of natural history and never works out a proposition of a theological character—not in a single line! And to philosophers, while God serves as premise and principle, the system does not derive its generative problematic from that fact. It is not that on which the system builders propose to work.

By showing that all things can be ordered, and that all orders can be set into relationship with one another, we transform method into message. The message of hierarchical classification is that many things really form a single thing, the many species a single genus, the many genera an encompassing and well-crafted cogent whole. Every time we speciate, we affirm that position; each successful labor of forming relationships among species, such as making them into a genus, or identifying the hierarchy of the species, proves it again. Furthermore, when we can show that many things are really one, or that one thing yields many (the reverse and confirmation of the former), we say in a fresh way a single immutable truth: the truth of this philosophy concerning the unity of all being in an orderly composition of all things within a single taxon.

To show how this works, I turn to a very brief sample of the Mishnah's authorship's sustained effort to demonstrate how many classes of things—relationships, circumstances, persons, places—really form one class. This supererogatory work of classification then works its way through the potentialities of chaos to explicit order. It is classification transformed from the how of intellection to the why and the what for and, above all, the what does it all mean.

The two matched and opposite propositions—many things are one, one thing encompasses many—complement each other, because together they provide a single, complete, and final judgment of the whole of being, social, natural, supernatural alike. Exegesis always is repetitive—and a sound exegesis of the systemic exegesis must then be equally so, everywhere explaining the same thing in the same way.

The sustained effort to demonstrate how many classes of things—actions, are demonstrated really to form one class bears implications for theology, but it is not a theological effort. The point is important nonetheless. Just as God, in creation, ordered all things, each in its class under its name, so in the Mishnah classification works its way through the potentialities of chaos to explicit order. As in the miracle of God's creation of the world in six days, here too is classification transformed from the *how* of intellection to the *why* and the *what for* and, above all, the *what-does-it-all-mean*.

The issue concerns nature, not supernature, and sorts out and sifts the everyday data of the here and the now. It will prove its points, therefore, by appeal to the palpable facts of creation, which everyone knows and can test. So recognition that one thing may fall into several categories and many things into a single one comes to expression, for the authorship of the Mishnah, in secular ways. One of the interesting ways is the analysis of the several taxa into which a single action may fall, with an account of the multiple consequences, such as the sanctions that are called into play, for a single action. The right taxonomy of persons, actions, and things will show the unity of all being by finding many things in one thing, and that forms the first of the two components of what I take to be the philosophy's teleology.

Makkot 3:9

There is one who ploughs a single furrow and is liable on eight counts of violating a negative commandment:

[Specifically, it is] he who (1) ploughs with an ox and an ass [Deuteronomy 22:10], which are (2, 3) both Holy Things, in the case of (4) [ploughing] Mixed Seeds in a vineyard [Deuteronomy 22:9], (5) in the Seventh Year [Leviticus 25:4], (6) on a festival [Leviticus 23:7] and who was both a (7) priest [Leviticus 21:1] and (8) a Nazirite [Numbers 6:6] [ploughing] in a grave-yard.

Hanania b. Hakhinai says, "Also: He is [ploughing while] wearing a garment of diverse kinds" [Leviticus 19:19, Deuteronomy 22:11].

They said to him, "This is not within the same class."

He said to them, "Also the Nazir is not within the same class [as the other transgressions]."

Here is a case in which more than a single set of flogging is called for. The felon is liable to 312 stripes, on the listed counts. The ox is sanctified to the altar, the ass to the Temple upkeep. Hanania's contribution is rejected since it has nothing to do with ploughing, and the sages' position is equally flawed. The main point, for our inquiry, is simple. The one action draws in its wake multiple consequences. Classifying a single thing as a mixture of many things then forms a part of the larger intellectual address to the nature of mixtures. But it yields a result that, in the analysis of an action, far transcends the metaphysical problem of mixtures, because it moves us toward the ontological solution of the unity of being.

So much for actions. How about substances? Can we say that diverse things, each in its own classification, form a single thing? Indeed so. Here is one example, among a great many candidates, taken from Mishnah-*Hallah*. The tractate takes as its theme the dough-offering to which the framers assume Numbers 15:17–21 refers: "of the first of your coarse meal you shall present a cake as an offering." The tractate deals with the definition of dough liable to the dough-offering, defining the bread, the process of separating dough-offering, and the liability of mixtures.

Hallah 1:1, 3

[Loaves of bread made from] five types [of grain] are subject to dough-offering:

(1) wheat, (2) barley, (3) spelt, (4) oats, and (5) rye;

lo, [loaves of bread made from] these [species] are subject to dough-offering,

and combine with each other [for the purpose of reckoning whether or not a batch of dough comprises the minimum volume subject to dough-offering (Mishnah *Hallah* 1:4, 2:6, Mishnah *Eduyyot* 1:2)].

and products of these species are forbidden for common use until Passover under the category of new produce [produce harvested before the waving of the first sheaf (Leviticus 23:14)].

And grasses of these species may not be reaped until the reaping of the first sheaf.

And if they took root prior to the waving of the first sheaf, the waving of the first sheaf releases them for common use;

but if they did not take root prior to the waving of the omer, they are forbidden for common use until the next omer.

Grain in the following categories is liable to dough-offering when made into dough but exempt from tithes:

Gleanings, forgotten sheaves, produce in the corner of a field, that which has been abandoned, first tithe from which heave offering of the tithe has been removed, second tithe, and that which is dedicated to the temple which has been redeemed, the leftover portion of grain which was harvested for the offering of the first sheaf, and grain which has not reached a third of its anticipated growth.

R. Eliezer says, "Grain which has not reached one third of its growth is exempt from dough-offering when made into dough."

Hallah 1:1 addresses the issue of whether or not five species of grain join together to produce dough of sufficient volume to incur liability to the dough-offering. Since they share in common the trait that they are capable of being leavened (*himus*), they do. So the genus encompasses all of the species, with the result that the classification process is neatly illustrated. "Joining together" or connection then forms a statement that these many things are one thing. *Hallah* 1:2 makes the same point about the five species. The interstitial cases at *Hallah* 1:3 are subject to ownership other than that of the farmer, but that fact does not change their status as to dough-offering. We take no account of the status with regard to ownership, past or present use as another type of offering, or the stage of growth of the grain whence the dough derives. This then forms the other side of the taxonomic labor: indicators that do not distinguish. The upshot is as I've said: many things are one thing; one rule applies to a variety of classes of grains.

The real interest in demonstrating the unity of being lies not in things but in abstractions, and among abstractions, as we have already seen in other connections, types of actions take center stage. As before, I present in evidence not episodic compositions, but the better part of a complete composite, a tractate, which, I maintain, is formulated to address the issue of method that I deem critical. For that purpose I point to Mishnah-tractate *Keritot*, because its governing purpose is to work out how many things are really one thing. This is accomplished by showing that the consequence of diverse actions is always one and the same. The issue of the tractate is the definition of occasions on which one is obligated to bring a sin-offering and a suspensive guilt-offering. The tractate lists those sins that are classified together by the differentiating criterion of intention. If one deliberately commits those sins, he is punished through extirpation. If it is done inadvertently, he brings a sin-offering. In case of doubt as to whether or not a sin has been committed (hence: inadvertently), he brings a suspensive guilt-offering. Leviticus 5:17-19 specifies that if one sins but does not know it, he brings a sin-offering or a guilt-offering. Then if he *has* sinned, a different penalty is invoked, with the suspensive guilt-offering at stake as well. While we have a sustained exposition of implications of facts that Scripture has provided, the tractate also covers problems of classification of many things as one thing, in the form of a single sin-offering for multiple sins, and that problem fills the bulk of the tractate.

Keritot 1:1, 2, 7, 3:2, 4

Thirty-six transgressions subject to extirpation are in the Torah. . . .

For those [transgressions] are people liable, for deliberately doing them, to the punishment of extirpation,
   and for accidentally doing them, to the bringing of a sin-offering,
   and for not being certain of whether or not one has done them, to a suspensive guilt-offering [Leviticus 5:17]—

"except for the one who imparts uncleanness to the sanctuary and its Holy Things,

"because he is subject to bringing a sliding scale offering (Leviticus 5:6-7, 11)," the words of R. Meir.

And sages say, "Also: [except for] the one who blasphemes, as it is said, 'You shall have one law for him that does anything unwittingly' (Numbers 15:29)—excluding the blasphemer, who does no concrete deed."

The woman who is subject to a doubt concerning [the appearance of] five fluxes,

or the one who is subject to a doubt concerning five miscarriages brings a single offering.

And she [then is deemed clean so that she] eats animal sacrifices.

And the remainder [of the offerings] are not an obligation for her.

[If she is subject to] five confirmed miscarriages,

or five confirmed fluxes,

she brings a single offering.

And she eats animal sacrifices.

But the rest [of the offerings, the other four] remain as an obligation for her [to bring at some later time]—

There was the following case: A pair of birds in Jerusalem went up in price to a golden denar.

Said Rabban Simeon b. Gamaliel, "By this sanctuary! I shall not rest tonight until they shall be at [silver] denars."

He entered the court and taught [the following law]:

"The woman who is subject to five confirmed miscarriages [or] five confirmed fluxes brings a single offering.

"And she eats animal sacrifices.

"And the rest [of the offerings] do not remain as an obligation for her."

And pairs of birds stood on that very day at a quarter-denar each [one one-hundredth of the former price].

[If] he ate [forbidden] fat and [again ate] fat in a single spell of inadvertence, he is liable only for a single sin offering,

[If] he ate forbidden fat and blood and remnant and refuse [of an offering] in a single spell of inadvertence, he is liable for each and every one of them.

This rule is more strict in the case of many kinds [of forbidden food] than of one kind.

And more strict is the rule in [the case of] one kind than in many kinds:

For if he ate a half-olive's bulk and went and ate a half-olive's bulk of a single kind, he is liable.

[But if he ate two half-olive's bulks] of two [different] kinds, he is exempt.

There is he who carries out a single act of eating and is liable on its account for four sin offerings and one guilt offering:

An unclean [lay] person who ate (1) forbidden fat, and it was (2) remnant (3) of Holy Things, and (4) it was on the Day of Atonement.

R. Meir says, "If it was the Sabbath and he took it out [from one domain to another] in his mouth, he is liable [for another sin offering]."

They said to him, "That is not of the same sort [of transgression of which we have spoken heretofore since it is not caused by eating]."

Keritot 1:7 introduces the case of classifying several incidents within a single taxon, so that one incident encompasses a variety of cases and therefore one penalty or sanction covers a variety of instances. That same conception is more amply set forth in Chapter 2 of the tractate. There we have lists of five who bring a single offering for many transgressions, five who bring a sliding scale offering for many incidents. Then in 3:1–3 we deal with diverse situations in which a man is accused of having eaten forbidden fat and therefore of owing a sin-offering. At Chapter 3:1 the issue is one of disjoined testimony. Do we treat as one the evidence of two witnesses? The debate concerns whether two cases form a single category. Sages hold that the cases are hardly the same, because there are differentiating traits. *Keritot* 3:2–3 shows us how we differentiate or unify several acts. We have several acts of transgression in a single spell of inadvertence; we classify them all as one action for purposes of the penalty. That at stake is the problem of classification, and how we invoke diverse taxic indicators is shown vividly at *Keritot* 3:2 in particular. Along these same lines are the issues of 3:4: "There is he who carries out a single act of eating and is liable on its account for four sin-offerings and one guilt-offering; there is he who carries out a single act of sexual intercourse and becomes liable on its account for six sin-offerings," with the first shown at 3:4 and the second at 3:5.

Showing that many things are really of one kind because they produce a single consequence—the same offering—proves inadequate. The reason is that that mode of argument by appeal to outcome or consequence ignores the traits of things, which the Mishnah's system, so it seems, deems paramount. So the approach provides a demonstration that bears three negative traits. First, it is formal, not substantive. Second, it is static, not dynamic, and so it fails to deal with movement and change, which is where diversity takes place. Finally, it addresses consequence, not essence, and that teleological proof leaves open the question of whether or not being as it is, and not only as they are meant to be, really forms a unity. For proving (or at least illustrating) that proposition, which demands a far more important place in the philosophical program meaning to state the unity of ontology, we have to find a different sort of proof altogether. It is one that appeals—not surprisingly!—to processes of classification of things *as they are,* as to their essence or being, not as to their consequences. And this draws us—as is our way—to ask whether there is a complete tractate that is devoted to showing the unity of *phenomenona.* Indeed there is, and an odd one at that. The survey of one of the strangest tractates in the Mishnah will show us how the intrinsic and inherent traits of things on their own prove the besought proposition.

The issue of how many things are one thing is spelled out in detail in Mishnah-tractate *Negaim.* This is not an easy tractate; it is a kind of geometry, very abstract conceptions being expressed in quite concrete notions. Mishnah-tractate *Negaim* takes up the issues of Leviticus 13 and 14, the uncleanness and purification of those affected by *saraat,* often mistranslated "leprosy." The principle of the unity of phenomena is not made articulate, but it does serve throughout the document. It does so through classification and then the joining of taxa. That fact shows us the teleology of the methods we have now identified as critical to the philosophical enterprise of Judaism, stating the proposition that is implicit in them.

Negaim 1:1–3

The appearances of plagues are two, which are four:
(1) A bright spot is as bright-white as snow. (2) And secondary to it is [a shade as white] as the lime of the Temple.
(3)"And the swelling is [as white] as the skin of an egg. (4) And secondary to it is [a shade as white] as white wool," the words of R. Meir.

And sages say, "(1) The swelling is [as white] as white wool. (2) Secondary to it is [a shade as white] as the skin of an egg."

"The [reddish] mixture which is in the snow—white is like wine mixed in snow.

"The [reddish] mixture in the lime is like the blood which is mixed in milk," the words of R. Ishmael.

R. Akiva says, (1.) "The reddishness which is in this and in this is like wine mixed in water.

(2.) "But that which is in snow—white is strong, and that which is in lime is duller than it."

These four appearances join together with one another—(1) to clear [of uncleanness], and (2) to certify [the sign to be unclean], and (3) to shut up [quarantine for a week]:

(3) To shut up: That which stands [unchanged] at the end of the first week.

(1) To declare clear: that which stands unchanged at the end of the second week.

(2) And to certify: That in which quick flesh or white hair appears,

(a) in the first instance, (b) at the end of the first week, (c) at the end of the second week, (d) after the clearance.

(2) To certify: That in which a spreading appears,

(a) at the end of the first week, (b) at the end of the second week, (c) after the clearance.

(2) To certify: That which turns entirely white (d) after the clearance.

To declare clear: That which turns entirely white after the certification or after the shutting up.

These are the appearances [colors] of plagues, upon which all plagues depend.

Negaim 1:1–6 presents a systematic classification of colors and shades that, appearing upon the skin, signify that uncleanness is present, and, further, addresses the issue of how these shades join together to form the affected space requisite for imparting uncleanness. The four colors or shades of white signify the presence of the skin disease in particular; they join together and form a common mixture. There are, further, three stages of inspection, and when they take place, color and other matters are inspected to find out whether diseased skin signifies uncleanness. The joining together means that if a bit of skin is of one shade and an adjacent bit is of another, the two are regarded as a single bright spot. A vast amount of information is held together, and the principal issues of classification and mixture are imposed upon it. Unity among diverse data is gained through appeal to standard taxa—for example, Israel as against the nations, the classifications within Israel of the several castes.

This is accomplished in Chapter 3 of the tractate. *Negaim* 3:1 classifies those subject to being affected by the skin uncleanness and those suitable for examining it. In the former are all persons except Gentiles and resident aliens; in the latter are all informed persons, with the priest in charge of stating the outcome. Another medium for unification of data, of course, is to show the simplicity of classifying extremely diverse phenomena. Formal traits—recurrent patterns—bear the substantive message, which is set forth with exceptional clarity.

Negaim 3:3–4

The skin of the flesh is made unclean within two weeks and by three tokens: with white hair, and with quick flesh, and with spreading.
With white hair and with quick flesh—
in the beginning, or by the end of the first week, or by the end of the second week, after the [declaration of] clearance.
And by spreading—
at the end of the first week, and at the end of the second week, after the clearance.
And it is made unclean within two weeks—
which are thirteen days.

The boil and the burning are made unclean in one week and with two tokens: with white hair and spreading.
With white hair—
in the beginning, at the end of the first week, after the clearance.
And with spreading—
at the end of a week, after the clearance.
And they are made unclean within one week—
which are seven days.

Negaim 3:3–8 take up the scriptural laws—in the model of the sample given here, which is repeated with great consistency throughout—and organize them in a set of classifications of the following taxic indicators: specification of the form of the ailment; the period of time over which it is inspected; the signs of contamination that may occur. These items are then set forth with respect to the skin of the flesh, *Negaim* 3:3, the boil and burning, 3:4, bald spot on the forehead and on the back of the head, clothing, and houses. Once more, as in Chapter 1 of the tractate, a sizable body of diverse information is reorganized into well-formed classifications.

The other half of the matter—the differentiation within a unity, once demonstrated, follows in *Negaim* Chapter 4. Here again we see the logical order in which a tractate investigates its topic. We first show unities, then differentiate within them. That underlines the polemic of the philosophy as a whole: everything is really one thing, even though one thing yields many things. One proposition without the other is simply incomplete. In the case at hand, once the taxic indicators have classified the various kinds of skin disease, the next step is to compare one species of the skin ailment to another, and this is accomplished at 4:1–3.

Negaim 4:1–2

There are [strict rules applying] to white hair which do not [apply] to spreading, and there are [rules applying] to spreading which do not [apply] to white hair.

For white hair (1) renders unclean in the first [inspection], and (2) renders unclean in any appearance [shade] of whiteness, and (3) no token of cleanness applies to it.

There are [strict rules applying] to spreading, for the spreading (1) renders unclean in any size whatever, and (2) renders unclean in all plagues, (3) [though] outside the plague [itself], which is not the case for white hair [which must be encompassed by the bright spot]—

There are [strict rules applying] to the quick flesh which do not apply to spreading, and there are [rules applying] to spreading which do not [apply] to quick flesh.

For the quick flesh (1) renders unclean in the first [inspection], and (2) renders unclean in any appearance [color], and (3) no token of cleanness applies to it.

There are [rules applying] to spreading, for the spreading (1) renders unclean in any size whatever, and (2) renders unclean in all plagues, (3) [though] outside the plague, which is not the case with quick flesh.

The relationship between an indicator and the skin concerning which the indicator testifies is compared from item to item. We begin with the skin of the flesh, that is, the point at which we started, with 3:3, affected by three indicators, white hair, quick flesh, and spreading. Then the impact of the indicator over a sequence of inspections is worked out, and then strict rules applying to one indicator but not another are specified. How a more perfect mode of taxonomy and hierarchical classification can have been devised I simply do not know. The whole of Chapter 4 (4:4–11) is captured here.

Negaim 4:5

A bright spot the size of a split bean—
and a streak extends from it—
if there is in it [the streak] the breadth of two hairs,
it [the streak] subjects it [the bright spot] to [the restrictions in respect of] white hair and spreading, but not to [that in respect of] the quick flesh.
Two bright spots,—
and a streak goes forth from one to the other—
if there is in it a breadth of two hairs,
it joins them together. And if not, it does not join them together.

The issue is whether a streak extending from a bright spot affects the bright spot. For example, if in the streak we have two white hairs, or if the spreading affects the streak but not the primary symptom, what is the rule? The answer is that if we have the stated breadth, sufficient for the growth of two hairs, the streak subjects the primary symptom to the restrictions which occur in the streak (which is then connected and through which a complete mixture is formed), and if not, it does not. The same point is made twice. Connection, classification—these yield a single point, that everything is subject to one coherent rule, and many things serve in their unity to demonstrate the essential unity of all things. That demonstration derives from the possibility of ordering many things in a single way.

However many times we construct problems for solution, theorems for demonstration, we return to that same point. How about humble things, things that ordinary people can understand, in a way in which the remote abstractions of Mishnah-tractate *Negaim* cannot be visualized? Let us turn to the corpse and the diverse fluids and substances that the corpse yields. Here we see in the application of reason and the practical uses of logic the one and the many, the many and the one. The laws about tents at Numbers 19:11–22 hold that if a corpse is located in a tent, whatever else is found underneath that same tent, even not touching the corpse, is contaminated by uncleanness produced by the corpse, which lasts for seven days and requires a purification rite.

Ohalot 2:1–2

These contaminate in the Tent: (1) the corpse, and (2) an olive's bulk [of flesh] from the corpse, and (3) an olive's bulk of corpse dregs, and (4) a ladleful of corpse mould; (5) the backbone, and the skull, and (6) a limb from the corpse, and (7) a limb from the living person on which is an appropriate amount of flesh;

(8) a quarter-qab of bones from the larger part of the frame [of the skeleton] or (9) from the larger number; and (10) the larger part of the frame or (11) the larger number of the corpse, even though there is not among them a quarter-qab, are unclean.

How much is the "larger number"? One hundred twenty-five.

(12) A quarter-log of blood and (13) a quarter-log of mingled blood from a single corpse [render unclean in a Tent].

R. Akiva says, "From two corpses."

The blood of a minor, all of which has exuded—

R. Akiva says, "Any amount."

And sages say, "A quarter-log."

An olive's bulk of a worm whether living or dead—

R. Eliezer declares unclean like its flesh.

And sages declare clean.

The ash of burned people—
R. Eliezer says, "Its measure is a quarter-qab."
And sages declare clean.
A ladleful and a bit more of grave dirt is unclean.
R. Simeon declares clean.
A ladleful of corpse mould which one kneaded with water is not a
connector for uncleanness.

On the surface, the issue of *Ohalot* 2:1–2 is the familiar one of
mixtures and connection. But underneath the proposition is that
many things are really one thing, producing a single consequence
not in everyday action—a given mode of execution, for instance—
but in the very nature of being, here, classification. The issue is
whether two species of the genus, that which contaminates by
reason of corpse uncleanness, join together to form the requisite
volume for conveying uncleanness; whether two corpses may
contribute to the formation of the requisite volume, and the like.
Must the requisite blood derive from a single corpse, or may blood
from two corpses combine, since they fall into a single taxon? There
is no clearer way of raising the question of the relationship of species
of the same genus than is precipitated by the odd categories at hand.

Can what was many things become one thing? Indeed so. The
problem of *Ohalot* 2:7 then is a special one: a bone the size of a
barleycorn which was divided into two parts; a quarter-qab of
crushed bones, in any one of which there is not a bone the size of
a barleycorn—that is to say, connection and mixtures once more.
More to the point, many things may be joined together by a
common function or by being subject to a common function.

Mishnah-tractate *Ohalot* 3:6–7 provides an ideal demonstration
of how, in action, being is made—shown to be—one. Let me
explain what is going to happen here. *Ohalot* 3:6–7 work out the
problem of how many things are one thing. At stake is how the tent
functions to spread about uncleanness that is underneath it. On the
surface, the issue is the definition of the tent. But the operative
question is how one tent relates to another beyond itself, beside
itself, or within itself. Scripture's rule is that a tent spreads corpse
uncleanness. But a tent may also interpose and prevent the spread
of corpse uncleanness. Then the issue is affording protection against
corpse uncleanness or interposition, and that, in the end, is a

question of whether we classify the tent as an autonomous and protected area or as an area that is joined with and part of a larger area. That is the basis for my judgment that at stake is the relationship of demarcated spaces, hence spatial mixtures.

Ohalot 3:6-7

An olive's bulk of a corpse—its opening is a handbreadth. And the corpse—its opening is four handbreadths.

To afford protection for the [other] openings against uncleanness.

But to give passage for the uncleanness [to go to an adjacent space], an opening of a handbreadth [suffices].

More than a handbreadth is like a corpse.

R. Yose says, "The backbone and the skull are like the corpse."

A cubic handbreadth introduces the uncleanness and interposes before the uncleanness.

How?

A drain which is arched under the house—

it is a handbreadth wide, and its outlet is a handbreadth wide—

uncleanness is in it—

the house is clean.

Uncleanness is in the house—

what is in it is clean,

for the way of the uncleanness is to exude, and it is not its way to seep in.

It is a handbreadth wide, and its outlet is not a handbreadth wide—

the uncleanness is in it—

the house is unclean.

Uncleanness is in the house

what is in it is clean,

for it is the way of the uncleanness to exude, and it is not its way to seep

It is not a handbreadth wide, and its outlet is not a handbreadth wide—

uncleanness is in it—

the house is unclean.

Uncleanness is in the house—

what is in it is unclean.

All the same is the hole dug by water or insects, or which saltpetre has eaten through—

and so a row of stones, and so a pile of beams.

R. Judah says, "Any Tent which is not made by man is no Tent."
But he agrees concerning the clefts and overhanging rocks.

The general rule then assigns an area that permits the joining in
two other ways distinct units of space: "An olive's bulk of a
corpse—its opening is a handbreadth. And the corpse—its opening
is four handbreadths. To afford protection for the [other] openings
against uncleanness. But to give passage for the uncleanness [to go
to an adjacent space], an opening of a handbreadth [suffices]." That
is, the specified areas of space serve to open two distinct spaces into
one another or to close off two areas of space from one another.

So much for the impalpable and invisible realm of classification
and status. There we can conjure, but cannot touch or feel or see,
the lines of structure and division. Order is imputed and imagined.
What about the visible world of space? Here we can frame a
question that permits a highly tangible representation of the
complexity of unity and diversity, the demonstration that one thing
encompasses many things, so many things form one thing. The
question is asked in this way: When is a field a field, and when is it
two or ten fields? That taxonomic problem of how many are
deemed one, or how one is many, is addressed at Mishnah-tractate
Peah, which concerns itself with giving to the poor the produce
abandoned at the corner of a field. We have to know what
constitutes a field, hence the question of when one thing is many
things, or when many things are one thing, framed in terms of
spatial relations:

Peah 2:1, 5; 3:5

And these [landmarks] establish [the boundaries of a field] for [purposes
of designating] peah:
(1) a river, (2) pond, (3) private road, (4) public road, (5) public path,
(6) private path that is in use in the hot season and in the rainy season, (7)
uncultivated land, (8) newly broken land, (9) and [an area sown with] a
different [type of] seed.
"And [as regards] one who harvests young grain [for use as fodder—the
area he harvests] establishes [the boundaries of a field]," the words of R.
Meir.

But sages say, "[The area he harvests] does not establish [the boundaries of a field], unless he has also ploughed [the stubble] under."

One who sows his field with [only] one type [of seed], even if he harvests [the produce] in two lots
   designates one [portion of produce as] *peah* [from the entire crop].
   If he sowed [his field] with two types [of seeds], even if he harvests [the produce] in only one lot,
   he designates two [separate portions of produce as] *peah,* [one from each type of produce].
   He who sows his field with two types of wheat—
   [if] he harvests [the wheat] in one lot, [he] designates one [portion of produce as] *peah.*
   [But if he harvests the wheat in] two lots, [he] designates two [portions of produce as] *peah.*

[Two] brothers who divided [ownership of a field which previously they had jointly owned]
   give two [separate portions of produce] as *peah* [each designates *peah* on behalf of the produce of his half of the field].
   [If] they return to joint ownership [of the field]
   [together] they designate one [portion of produce] as *peah* [on behalf of the entire field].
   Two [men] who [jointly] purchased a tree
   [together] designate one [portion of produce] as *peah* [on behalf of the entire tree]—
   But if one purchased the northern [half of the tree], and the other purchased the southern [half of the tree],
   the former designates *peah* by himself, and the latter designates *peah* by himself. . . .

The principle of division rests upon the farmer's attitude and actions toward a field. If the farmer harvests an area as a single entity, that action indicates his attitude or intentionality in regard to that area and serves to mark it as a field. For each patch of grain the householder reaps separately, a *peah*-share must be designated; the action indicates the intentionality to treat the area as a single field. But natural barriers intervene; rivers or hills also may mark off a field's boundaries, whatever the farmer's action and therefore a priori intentionality or attitude. In classifying an area of ground as a field, therefore, there is an interplay between the givens of the physical traits and the farmer's attitude, confirmed by action.

If then many things become one thing, how about the one thing that yields the many? If we can show that a single classification may be *subdivided*, then the unity of the many in the one is demonstrated from a fresh angle. If so, the systemic contention concerning the fundamental and essential unity of all being finds reinforcement. That the question is faced may be shown, as usual in so coherent a piece of writing as the Mishnah, at a variety of passages, for instance, those that ask, when are many actions classified as a single action, or a single action as many. But, more to the point, let us turn now to a very concrete reflection on the nature of actions and differentiating among them.

Nazir 6:4–5

A Nazir who was drinking wine all day long is liable only on one count.

[If] they said to him, "Don't drink it! Don't drink it!" and he continues drinking, he is liable on each and every count [of drinking].

[If] he was cutting his hair all day long, he is liable only on a single count.

[If] they said to him, "Don't cut it! Don't cut it!" and he continued to cut his hair, he is liable for each and every count [of cutting].

[If] he was contracting corpse uncleanness all day long, he is liable on only one count.

If they said to him, "Don't contract corpse uncleanness! Don't contract corpse uncleanness!" and he continued to contract corpse uncleanness, he is liable for each and every count.

Three things are prohibited to a Nazir: [corpse] uncleanness, cutting the hair, and anything which goes forth from the grapevine.

A more strict rule applies to corpse uncleanness and haircutting than applies to that which comes forth from the grapevine.

For corpse uncleanness and haircutting cause the loss of the days already observed, but [violating the prohibition against] that which goes forth from the vine does not cause the loss of the days already observed.

A more strict rule applies to that which goes forth from the vine than applies to corpse uncleanness and haircutting.

For that which goes forth from the vine allows for no exception, but corpse uncleanness and haircutting allow for exceptions,

in the case of [cutting the hair for] a religious duty and in the case of finding a neglected corpse [with no one else to provide for burial, in which case, the Nazir is absolutely required to bury the corpse].

A more strict rule applies to corpse uncleanness than to haircutting.

For corpse uncleanness causes the loss of all the days previously observed and imposes the liability for an offering.

But haircutting causes the loss of only thirty days and does not impose liability for an offering.

At *Nazir* 6:4 we take up the issue of disjoined actions, for each of which one is liable, when these actions are of a single species. What distinguishes one action from another, when all are of the same species, is that one is made aware each time he does the prohibited action that he is forbidden to do so. If he is not made aware, then all of the actions form a single sustained action, and he is liable on only one count. This interesting conception then imposes upon the differentiation of actions the consideration of intentionality: the man now knows that the particular action he is about to undertake is prohibited. Hence it seems to me a case in which we invoke intentionality in the work of the classification of actions (= counts of culpability). What is at stake in the issue? It is the application of hierarchical classification, which, as we know, forms the goal of the philosophy's method of classification. So we see the unity of philosophical medium and philosophical message. *Nazir* 6:5 takes the facts of Scripture and forms of them a composition of hierarchical classification, in which the taxic indicators are laid out in accord with a single program.

I have repeatedly claimed that the recognition that one thing becomes many does not challenge but rather confirms the philosophy of the unity of all being. Why do I insist on that proposition? The reason is simple. If we can show that differentiation flows from within what is differentiated—that is, from the intrinsic or inherent traits of things—then we confirm that at the heart of things is a fundamental ontological being, single, cogent, and simple, that is capable of diversification, yielding complexity and diversity. The upshot is to be stated with emphasis: *The fact that diversity in species or diversification in actions follows orderly lines confirms the claim that there is that single point from which many lines come forth.* Carried out in proper order—(1) the many form one thing, and (2) one thing yields many—the demonstration then leaves no doubt as to the truth of the matter. Ideally, therefore, we shall argue from the simple to the complex, showing that the one yields the many, two yields four.

Shabbat 1:1

[Acts of] transporting objects from one domain to another, [which violate] the Sabbath, (1) are two, which [indeed] are four [for one who is] inside, (2) and two which are four [for one who is] outside.

How so?

[If on the Sabbath] the beggar stands outside and the householder inside,

[and] the beggar stuck his hand inside and put [a beggar's bowl] into the hand of the householder,

or if he took [something] from inside it and brought it out,

the beggar is liable, the householder is exempt.

[If] the householder stuck his hand outside and put [something] into the hand of the beggar,

or if he took [something] from it and brought it inside,

the householder is liable, and the beggar is exempt.

[If] the beggar stuck his hand inside, and the householder took [something] from it,

or if [the householder] put something in it and he [the beggar] removed it,

both of them are exempt.

[If] the householder put his hand outside and the beggar took [something] from it,

or if [the beggar] put something into it and [the householder] brought it back inside,

both of them are exempt.

1:1 classifies diverse circumstances of transporting objects from private to public domain. The purpose is to assess the rules that classify diverse arrangements as culpable or exempt from culpability. The operative point is that a prohibited action is culpable only if one and the same person commits the whole of the violation of the law. If two or more people share in the single action, neither of them is subject to punishment. At stake therefore is the conception that one thing may be many things, and if that is the case, then culpability is not incurred by any one actor.

The consequence of showing that one thing is many things is set forth with great clarity in the consideration not of the actor but of the action. One class of actions is formed by those that violate the sanctity of the Sabbath. Do these form many subdivisions, and, if so, what difference does it make? Here is a famous passage that shows how a single class of actions yields multiple and complex speciation while remaining one:

Shabbat 7:1–2

A general rule did they state concerning the Sabbath:

Whoever forgets the basic principle of the Sabbath and performed many acts of labor on many different Sabbath days is liable only for a single sin-offering.

He who knows the principle of the Sabbath and performed many acts of labor on many different Sabbaths is liable for the violation of each and every Sabbath.

He who knows that it is the Sabbath and performed many acts of labor on many different Sabbaths is liable for the violation of each and every generative category of labor.

He who performs many acts of labor of a single type is liable only for a single sin-offering.

The generative categories of acts of labor [prohibited on the Sabbath] are forty less one:

(1) he who sews, (2) ploughs, (3) reaps, (4) binds sheaves, (5) threshes, (6) winnows, (7) selects [fit from unfit produce or crops], (8) grinds, (9) sifts, (10) kneads, (11) bakes;

(12) he who shears wool, (13) washes it, (14) beats it, (15) dyes it;

(16) spins, (17) weaves,

(18) makes two loops, (19) weaves two threads, (20) separates two threads;

(21) ties, (22) unties,

(23) sews two stitches, (24) tears in order to sew two stitches;

(25) he who traps a deer, (26) slaughters it, (27) flays it, (28) salts it, (29) cures its hide, (30) scrapes it, and (31) cuts it up;

(32) he who writes two letters, (33) erases two letters in order to write two letters; (34) he who builds, (35) tears down;

(36) he who puts out a fire, (37) kindles a fire;

(38) he who hits with a hammer; (39) he who transports an object from one domain to another—

lo, these are the forty generative acts of labor less one.

Now we see how the fact that one thing yields many things confirms the philosophy of the unity of all being. For the many things all really are one thing, here the intrusion into sacred time of actions that do not belong there. Mishnah-tractate *Shabbat* 7:1-2 presents a parallel to the discussion, in *Sanhedrin*, of how many things can be shown to be one thing and to fall under a single rule, and how one thing may be shown to be many things and to invoke multiple consequences. It is that interest at *Shabbat* 7:1 which accounts for the inclusion of 7:2, and the exposition of 7:2 occupies much of the tractate that follows. Accordingly, just as at Mishnah-tractate *Sanhedrin* the specification of the diverse sins or felonies that are penalized in a given way shows us how many things are one thing and then draws in its wake the specification of those many things, so here we find a similar exercise. It is one of classification, working in two ways, then: the power of a unifying taxon, the force of a differentiating and divisive one. The list of the acts of labor then gives us the categories of work, and performing any one of these constitutes a single action in violation of the Sabbath.

How, exactly, do these things work themselves out? If one does not know that the Sabbath is incumbent upon him, then whatever he does falls into a single taxon. If he knows that the Sabbath exists and violates several Sabbath days in succession, what he does falls into another taxon. If one knows that the Sabbath exists in principle and violates it in diverse ways, such as through different types of prohibited acts of labor, then many things become still more differentiated. The consideration throughout, then, is how to assess whether something is a single or multiple action as to the reckoning of the consequence.

I have repeatedly pointed to the philosophical unity of mode of argument, medium of expression, and fundamental proposition. In this connection let us turn back to our consideration of the rules of speciation. These form the methodological counterpart to the proposition that one thing yields many things. Here is the consequence, in the context of the exposition of the one and the many, of the rule of sub- and superspeciation:

Shabbat 10:6

He who pares his fingernails with one another, or with his teeth,

so too [if he pulled out the hair of] his (1) head, (2) moustache, or (3) beard—

and so she who (1) dresses her hair, (2) puts on eye shadow, or (3) rouges her face—

R. Eliezer declares liable [for doing so on the Sabbath].

And sages prohibit [doing so] because of [the principle of] Sabbath rest.

He who picks [something] from a pot which has a hole [in the bottom] is liable.

[If he picks something from a pot] which has no hole [in the bottom], he is exempt.

And R. Simeon exempts him on this account and on that account.

The interest in the classification of acts of labor draws attention, at *Shabbat* 10:6, to the lesson of superspeciation. We make a distinction between a derivative of the generative categories of prohibited acts, commission of which invokes a penalty, and an act that is not to be done by reason of the general principle of "Sabbath rest" but is not culpable under the list of thirty-nine specifically prohibited acts of labor. From superspeciation—acts that cannot be speciated but that fall into the genus of prohibited deeds—we move, in *Shabbat* Chapters 12 through 16, to the subspecies of the thirty-nine categories of prohibited acts of labor. Here we ask about the extent to which one must perform a prohibited act of labor in order to be subject to liability; Chapter 12 addresses building, ploughing, and writing; Chapter 13 proceeds to weaving and hunting (one who completes an action is liable, one who does not is exempt; one who does not intend by his action to violate the Sabbath is not liable and one who does intend to violate the Sabbath is liable; if two people together do a single act of prohibited labor, neither is liable); Chapter 15 moves on to knot-tying; Chapter 16, to saving things from the fire even though doing so requires moving objects across the boundary between private and public domain.

The Sabbath exposition appears so perfectly apt for the present proposition that readers may wonder whether the authorship of the Mishnah could accomplish that same wonder of concision of complex thought more than a single time. Joining rhetoric, logic, and specific (no longer general, methodological) proposition transforms thought into not merely expository prose but poetry. Have I given a proof consisting of one case? Quite to the contrary, the document contains a plethora of exercises of the same kind. My final demonstration of the power of speciation in demonstrating the opposite, namely, the generic unity of species and the hierarchy that orders them, derives from the treatment of oaths, to which we now turn. The basic topical program of Mishnah-tractate *Shabuot* responds systematically to the potpourri of subjects covered by Leviticus Chapters 5 and 6 within the (to the priestly author) unifying rubric of those who bring a guilt-offering. Leviticus 5:1–6 concerns oaths, an oath of testimony, one who touches something unclean in connection with the Temple cult, and finally, one who utters a rash oath.

Shabuot 1:1–2; 2:1

Oaths are of two sorts, which yield four subdivisions.

Awareness of [having sinned through] uncleanness is of two sorts, which yield four subdivisions.

Transportation [of objects from one domain to the other] on the Sabbath is of two sorts, which yield four subdivisions.

The symptoms of *negas* are of two sorts, which yield four subdivisions.

In any case in which there is awareness of uncleanness at the outset and awareness [of uncleanness] at the end but unawareness in the meantime—lo, this one is subject to bringing an offering of variable value.

[If] there is awareness [of uncleanness] at the outset but no apprehension [of uncleanness] at the end, a goat which [yields blood to be sprinkled] within [in the Holy of Holies], and the Day of Atonement suspend [the punishment],

until it will be made known to the person, so that he may bring an offering of variable value.

Awareness of uncleanness is of two sorts, which yield four subdivisions.

(1) [If] one was made unclean and knew about it, then the uncleanness left his mind, but he knew [that the food he had eaten was] Holy Things,

(2) the fact that the food he had eaten was Holy Things left his mind, but he knew about [his having contracted] uncleanness,

(3) both this and that left his mind, but he ate Holy Things without knowing it and after he ate them, he realized it—

lo, this one is liable to bring an offering of variable value.

(1) [If] he was made unclean and knew about it, and the uncleanness left his mind, but he remembered that he was in the sanctuary;

(2) the fact that he was in the sanctuary left his mind, but he remembered that he was unclean,

(3) both this and that left his mind, and he entered the sanctuary without realizing it, and then when he had left the sanctuary, he realized it—

lo, this one is liable to bring an offering of variable value.

Shabuot 1:1–7 and 2:1–5 accomplish the speciation of oaths, on the one side, and uncleanness in regard to the cult, on the other. That work of speciation then joins two utterly disparate subjects, oaths and uncleanness, and in doing so shows a unity of structure that forms a metaphysical argument for the systemic proposition on the unity of being. One does so in a way that is now to be predicted. It is by showing that many things are one thing. When the priestly author joined the same subjects, it was because a single offering was involved for diverse and distinct sins or crimes. When the Mishnaic author does, it is because a single inner structure sustains these same diverse and distinct sins or crimes. Comparing the priestly with the Mishnah's strategy of exposition underlines the remarkable shift accomplished by our philosophers. Their power of formulation— rhetoric and logic together—of course, works to demonstrate through the medium the message that these enormously diverse subjects in fact can be classified within a simple taxonomic principle: that there are two species to a genus, and two subspecies to each species, and these are readily determined by appeal to fixed taxic indicators. An abstract statement of the rule of classification (and, it must follow, also hierarchization) will have yielded less useful intellectual experience than the remarkably well-balanced concrete exemplification of the rule, and that is precisely what we have in Mishnah-tractate *Shabuot* Chapters 1 and 2.

That process of speciation and subspeciation is where the uniformity of oaths is established, with the consequence, given our starting point, that many things are really one thing, for, as we see at the outset, they come from one thing.

Shabuot 3:1–2, 8–9, 11

Oaths are of two sorts, which yield four subdivisions.
(1) "I swear I shall eat," and (2) ". . . I shall not eat,"
(3) ". . . that I ate," and (4) ". . . that I didn't eat."
"[If one said], 'I swear I won't eat,' and he ate anything [in any volume] whatsoever, he is liable," the words of R. Akiva.

They said to R. Akiva, "Where have we found that someone who eats anything in any negligible volume is liable, that this one should be deemed liable?"

Said to them R. Akiva, "And where have we found that one who merely speaks has to bring an offering?"

"I swear that I won't eat," and he ate and drank—he is liable on only one count.

"I swear that I won't eat and drink," and he ate and drank—he is liable on two counts.

"I swear I won't eat,"—
and he ate a piece of bread made of wheat, a piece of bread made of barley, and a piece of bread made of spelt, he is liable on one count only.

"I swear that I won't eat a piece of bread made of wheat, a piece of bread made of barley, and a piece of bread made of spelt," and he ate—
he is liable on each and every count.

What is a vain oath?
[If] one has taken an oath to differ from what is well-known to people.
If he said (1) concerning a pillar of stone that it is made of gold,
(2) concerning a man that he is a woman,
(3) concerning a woman that she is a man—

[if] one has taken an oath concerning something which is impossible—
(1) ". . . if I did not see a camel flying in the air . . ."
(2) ". . . if I did not see a snake as thick as the beam of an olive press . . . ,"
(3) [if] he said to witnesses, "Come and bear witness of me,"
[and they said to him,] "We swear that we shall not bear witness for you"—
[if] he took an oath to nullify a commandment—
(1) not to build a *sukkah*, (2) not to take *lulab* and (3) not to put on phylacteries—
this is a vain oath,
on account of the deliberate making of which one is liable for flogging, and on account of the inadvertent making of which one is exempt [from all punishment].

"I swear that I shall eat this loaf of bread," "I swear that I shall not eat it"—
the first statement is a rash oath, and the second is a vain oath.
[If] he ate it, he has violated a vain oath.
[If] he did not eat it, he has violated a rash oath.

[The law governing] a vain oath applies (1) to men and women, (2) to those who are not related and to those who are related, (3) to those who are suitable [to bear witness] and to those who are not suitable [to bear witness],
(4) before a court and not before a court.
(5) [But it must be stated] by a man out of his own mouth.
And they are liable for deliberately taking such an oath to flogging, and for inadvertently taking such an oath, one is exempt [from all punishment].
All the same are this oath and that oath:
he who was subjected to an oath by others is liable.
How so?
[If] one said, "I did not eat today, and I did not put on phylacteries today,"
[and his friend said,] "I impose an oath on you [that that is so],"
and he said, "Amen,"
he is liable.

The speciation and subspeciation of oaths occupies the rest of the tractate. Not only so, but we now find out what is at stake in the matter. It has to do with the number of counts for which one is liable, which is to say, the division of a given action or statement into its components and the identification of each completed action or statement, that is, the number of counts of liability. All of this is entirely familiar. It is the point at which we started. But here that point emerges in the analysis of the language one has used in the oath at hand. Since one has taken one oath, there is one point of liability. But since he has in the oath specified two or more actions, he is liable for violating the oath as to each of those actions. Thus at Mishnah-tractate *Shabuot* 3:1ff., we have the speciation of oaths into four types, then the demonstration of the subspeciation of a given type by appeal to the language that is used. *Shabuot* 3:1–6 go over oaths in general. *Shabuot* 3:2 shows how one thing yields many things. *Shabuot* 3:7–11 deals with the vain oath, differentiating that from the rash oath. These show us the model that is followed, with variations required by the subject matter, for the rest.

Once we reflect on the simple fact that nearly the whole of Mishnah-tractate *Negaim* and the entirety of Mishnah-tractate *Shabuot* perform precisely the same tasks in exactly the same way, we realize how fully and broadly our authorship has accomplished its philosophical goal. It has shown that any topic allows for the same demonstration of the same proposition in a single way, and that means everything really does fall into one simple pattern. The very diversity of the topical program of the Mishnah then forms on its own an argument in behalf of the philosophy's single proposition. For if one wants to show that many things are really one, and that one thing yields many things, the best way to do it is to show that you can say the same thing about many things—the more, the better.

To conclude: the species point to the genus, all classes to one class, and all taxa properly hierarchized then rise to the top of the structure and the system, forming one taxon. So all things ascend to and reach one thing. All that remains is for the theologian to define that one thing: God. But that is a step that the philosophers of the Mishnah did not take. Perhaps it was because they did not think they had to. But I think there is an altogether different reason. It is because they were in fact philosophers. And to philosophers, as I said at the outset, God serves as premise and principle (and whether or not it is one God or many gods, a unique being or a being that finds a place in a class of similar beings, hardly is germane!), and philosophy serves not to demonstrate principles or to explore premises, but to analyze the unknown, to answer important questions.

In such an enterprise the premise, God, turns out to be merely instrumental, and the given principle, so to be merely interesting. But for philosophers, intellectuals, God can live not in the details, but in the unknowns, in the as-yet unsolved problem and the unresolved dilemma. So I think that in the Mishnah, God lives, so to speak, in the excluded middle, is revealed in the interstitial case, is made known through the phenomena that form a single phenomenon, is perceived in the one that is many, is encountered in the many that are one. For that is the dimension of being—that, so I claim, immanental and sacramental dimension of being—that defines for this philosophy its statement of ultimate concern, its recurrent point of tension. That then is the urgent question, the ineluctable and self-evidently truthful answer: God in the form, God in the order, God in the structure, God in the heights, God at the head of the great chain of well-ordered being, in its proper hierarchy. True, God is premise, scarcely mentioned. But it is because God's name does not have to be mentioned when the whole of the order of being says that name, and only that name, and always that name, the Name unspoken because it is always in the echo, the silent, thin voice, the numinous in all phenomena of relationship: the interstitial God of the Mishnah. Before we turn to how the successor sages of the Talmud of the Land of Israel restated matters, let us see how God appears in the Mishnah.

2

God as Presence and as Person

$\mathbf{I}$t is one thing to find God as premise of the law. It is quite another to locate evidence of the portrayal of God as a presence within the processes of exposition and, more important, application of the law. The Hebrew word generally translated "Presence," *Shekhinah,* does occur in the Mishnah, if in only one passage:

Sanhedrin 6:5

Said R. Meir, "When a human being is in distress, as to the Presence of God, what does [its] tongue say . . . ?"

The premise is that God suffers along with human beings. It follows that, in general, God is understood not merely as a philosophical premise, such as we have now seen, or even as a source of authority, but also as a presence.

But the picture painted by the authorship of the Mishnah in general leaves a quite different impression. Like eighteenth-century Deists, the Mishnah's philosophers focus upon the government by the rule and law that God set forth in the Torah. Taking slight interest in God's particular intervention into the smooth application of the now-paramount regularities of the law, that authorship rarely represented God as an immediate—and by definition irregular—presence, let alone person. That sort of intervention by God is invoked only in one instance known to me, as I shall suggest in a moment. The Mishnah's authorship rarely decided a rule or a case by appealing to God's presence and choice particular to that rule or case.

That is to say, God as not premise but immediate presence does not often play an active role in the Mishnah's processes of decision-making. To take two stunning examples, in the entire division of Purities, which encompasses more than a quarter of the Mishnah in volume, I cannot point to a single passage in which God's presence forms a consideration of cleanness or uncleanness, susceptibility or insusceptibility to uncleanness, in the statement or application of a rule. The rules of susceptibility to and contracting of uncleanness, as well as those of removing that uncleanness, work themselves out with appeal to God's will or person. That is the case, even though the division attends to laws meant by the account of the priestly authorship of Leviticus and Numbers to protect the cult from the danger of uncleanness. A survey of the civil code presented in the tractates *Baba Qamma, Baba Mesia,* and *Baba Batra,* covering the transactions of commerce, real estate, torts, damages, labor law, and the like, that, in the aggregate, correspond to civil law in our own society, yields not a single appeal to God's presence or God's ad hoc intervention into a case. All things are governed by regularities and norms, such that God has no place in the everyday world of mortals' exchanges. While God forms the prevailing premise of discourse, that fact makes slight difference in what is said. The Mishnah's is a God of philosophers.

The full weight of the nature of the Mishnah's portrayal of the character of divinity will make its mark only when we have taken the measure of both the Yerushalmi and the Bavli Talmud. There the contrast between God as essentially a premise of all being and God as an active personality engaged in everyday transactions with specific persons will lend immediacy to these general observations. But even in the Mishnah, an exception to the rule of God as formal premise of being highlights the rule.

The exception, which shows us how things might have been, is represented by the ordeal imposed on a woman accused of adultery (tractate *Sotah*). There, it is presupposed, God does intervene on an ad hoc basis. Since pentateuchal writings know many other cases in which God is expected to intervene, case by case (for example, the death of the sons of Aaron at Leviticus 16:1), we may wonder why the Mishnah's authorship has chosen this one among all possibilities for immediate divine participation in the administration of the law. But that exception does prove the rule that God has defined the norms and does not thereafter intervene in their application and execution. For no other ordeal relying upon God's engagement in a decision-making process appears in the Mishnah's system. The Mishnah moreover rarely appeals to heavenly sanctions, but commonly, in practical matters, to human ones. The penalties catalogued in tractate *Sanhedrin,* for example, encompass this-worldly recompense for this-worldly sin.

True enough, the Mishnah's system knows penalties inflicted by Heaven, catalogued in the tractate on *Keritot,* grounds for extirpation or premature death. But the same authorship invokes heavenly intervention only by rule and law, not by individual case. The penalty of extirpation is governed by the same regularities as is the forfeiture of property in payment of a penalty. The same system holds even for denial of a share in the world to come—on grounds important to Heaven and assessed by Heaven, namely, denying that the resurrection of the dead derives from the Torah, denying that the Torah comes from Heaven, and Epicureanism. These are not matters subject to human inquisition but rather to God's knowledge. But here too there is a single law which applies throughout. God plays a role in judging a specific case only in the matter of the accused wife. In general, therefore, God's presence in the system of the Mishnah, while everywhere a premise and an implicit fact, plays only a limited and generally passive role.

Quite to the contrary, it is the will and intention of the human being that form the variable. God is the norm and the given; God's will and law, revealed in the Torah, is the ubiquitous fact. For the philosophers behind the Mishnah, therefore, God's presence forms part of the reliable structure of existence. It is the human will that is unpredictable, and that imparts to the Mishnah's system its movement, energy, and dynamism. That it is human and not divine intentionality that defines the system's principal problematic is shown, paradoxically, in its presentation of the cult on everyday occasions and of the rules for the upkeep of the cult. Here the variable is, on the one side, the attitude and intention of the *sacrifier,* the owner, who designates a beast as holy, and on the other, of the *sacrificer,* the priest, who kills the beast and sprinkles the blood on the altar. God's presence at the cult, God's enjoyment of the smell of the smoke of meat burning on the holy barbeque—

these form no point of discourse at all, though of course Scripture has assured them a central place. We look in vain in the principal tractates that take up the disposition of offerings, *Zebahim* and *Menahot,* and in the ones that define what is deemed sanctified or designated for use on the altar, such as *Meilah* and *Temurah,* for God's act of intervention or a divine indication that one rule rather than some other applies to a given case. Validation or invalidation of an act of designation of a beast as holy or an act of sacrifice depends upon the intention of the sacrifier or the sacrificer, not upon the intervention of God. The rules are what they are, and they apply as they apply.

Always present, invariably a participant in the sacrifice as principal beneficiary of the smoke of the burning meat, yet in the exposition of the rules of the Mishnah God is no presence in the cult. That fact is shown in a striking way by the prevailing power of fixed rules rather than the engagement of "the sacred" in specific cases. The statement is simple:

Zebahim 9:1

"The altar consecrates what is appropriate to the altar" and does not consecrate what is inappropriate to it.

The altar sanctifies that which is appropriate to it.

R. Joshua says, "Whatever is appropriate to the altar fires, if it has gone up [onto the fires], should not go down, since it is said, 'This is the burnt offering—that which goes up on the hearth on the altar' (Leviticus 6:9)—

"Just as the burnt offering, which is appropriate to the altar fires, if it has gone up, should not go down, so whatever is appropriate to the altar fires, if it has gone up, should not go down."

Rabban Gamaliel says, "Whatever is appropriate to the altar, if it has gone up, should not go down, as it is said, 'This is the burnt offering on the hearth on the altar' (Leviticus 6:2)—

"Just as the burnt offering, which is appropriate to the altar, if it has gone up, should not go down, so whatever is appropriate to the altar, if it has gone up, should not go down."

The difference between the opinion of Rabban Gamaliel and the opinion of R. Joshua is only the blood and the drink offerings.

For Rabban Gamaliel says, "They should not [having been placed on the altar] go down."

And R. Joshua says, "They should go down."

R. Simeon says, "[If] (1) the animal sacrifice is valid and the drink offerings invalid, (2) the drink offerings valid and the animal sacrifice invalid, [or] even if (3) this and that are invalid—the animal sacrifice should not go down, and the drink offerings should go down."

What that means is that merely being placed upon the altar does not consecrate a beast that is not an acceptable sacrifice, such as a chicken or a turtle. That rule imposing totally rational considerations of fixed law in the place of unpredictable intervention of power beyond all rule would surprise Scripture, which understood that merely touching the altar imparted holiness to whatever touched it: "Whatever touches the altar shall become consecrated" (Exodus 29:37). It goes without saying, therefore, that here there is no counterpart in the entirety of the civil law to the ordeal, at which God is required to give a specification of the pertinent rule or decision for a given case.

That is not to suggest as a final judgment that the Mishnah's God is to be compared to that of the Deists, or that God is merely the one who made the watch and wound it up to run on its own forever, more or less. In the Mishnah we deal with a system in no way comparable to that of the eighteenth-century philosophers' God. The reason is simple. In the Mishnah we deal with God not merely as the rule maker and premise of a system, but as a presence. For the Mishnah's is a God who hears prayer and sometimes responds to human wishes and requests. God, moreover, is surely present in the Temple, as the Mishnah's authorship states in diverse ways, even though in the account of the cult in tractate *Tamid* God plays no role in the picture of the conduct of the cult as it is carried out every day.

The generative force of the Mishnah's system—the active power that makes the system work, frames its questions, and dictates its answers—is the human attitude and intention. That is the point at which, ordinarily, the Mishnah also invokes God's presence. That is to say, God's presence forms the presupposition of those rules that attend to human attitude during the performance of certain religious actions, such as the recitation of obligatory prayers. For example, the obligation to recite the *Shema* encompasses the requirement "to direct one's heart," which is to say, to recite the required words with the intention of fulfilling one's duty to recite those words (*Berakhot* 2:1). One's attitude is taken into account in diverse other ways, as in not reciting the *Shema* under circumstances that will prevent one from forming the right attitude, such as when one has to bury a deceased relative (*Berakhot* 3:1). So too, when one is reciting the Prayer (the Eighteen Benedictions), it must be in a sober attitude (*Berakhot* 5:1), and particular piety requires an hour of inner preparation, "that they may direct their heart toward God."

Berakhot 5:1–5

One may stand to pray only in a solemn frame of mind.

The early pious ones used to tarry one hour [before they would] pray, so that they could direct their hearts to the Omnipresent.

[While one is praying] even if the king greets him, he may not respond.

And even if a serpent is entwined around his heel, he may not interrupt [his prayer].

They refer to the "wonder of the rain" in [the blessing concerning] "the resurrections of the dead," [the second blessing in the Eighteen Benedictions].

And they ask for the rains in "the blessings of the years," [the ninth blessing],

And [they insert] *habdalah* in [the blessing which concludes] "endower of knowledge," [the fourth blessing].

R. Akiva says, "One says it as a fourth blessing unto itself."

R. Eliezer says, "[One says it] in the 'thanksgiving,'" [the eighteenth blessing].

[As for] one who says, "May thy mercy reach the nest of a bird" or "For good may your name be mentioned," "We give thanks, we give thanks"—they silence him.

[As for] one who comes before the ark [to recite the liturgy on behalf of the congregation] and erred—let another go before [the ark] in his place.

And [the one designated as a replacement] may not decline at this time.

Whence does [the replacement] begin?

At the beginning of the blessing in which the [previous] one erred.

One who goes before the ark [to lead the prayer] shall not answer "Amen" after the [blessing of the] priests.

Because [he might become] confused [and not know where to begin again].

And [even] if there is no priest present besides himself [the leader], he should not raise his hands [as normally is done by priests who recite the priestly blessing],

But if he is sure that he can raise his hands [to recite the priestly blessing] and return to his prayer, he is permitted [to do so].

He who prays and errs—it is a bad sign for him.

And if he is a communal agent, [who prays on behalf of the whole congregation], it is a bad sign for them that appointed him.

[This is on the principle that] a man's agent is like [the man] himself.

They said concerning R. Haninah b. Dosa, "When he would pray for the sick he would say 'This one shall live' or 'That one shall die.' "

They said to him, "How do you know?"

He said to them, "If my prayer flows easily in my mouth, I know that it is accepted [and the person will live].

"But if not, I know that it is rejected [and the person will die]."

It must follow that there is a presence to assess the recitation of the correct words with the correct attitude. That presence is not material; one fulfills the obligation even though the words are not said sufficiently loud to be heard, even by the one who says them (*Berakhot* 2:3). But it is physical, in the sense that God is assumed to be located in one place rather than in some other. Accordingly, one recites prayers facing a particular location, namely, Jerusalem, and if one cannot do so in a physical way, at least one does so in the heart, directing the heart "toward the Holy of Holies" (*Berakhot* 4:6). That God is conceived to be located in the Holy of Holies is underlined by the rule that one should not conduct oneself in an inappropriate way while opposite the Temple's eastern gate, which faces the Holy of Holies (*Berakhot* 9:5). It goes without saying that God hears and answers statements made in any language, not only in Hebrew, although Hebrew is the holy and preferred language for certain formulas (*Sotah* 7:1–2).

God's presence is signified by awareness of the character of the occasion as well, such as the number and splendor of those present. Rules covering the recitation of prayers took account of the size and importance of those present on the occasion. If three are present for the Grace after Meals, one begins, "Bless the one of whose bounty we have partaken"; if there are ten, "Bless our God . . . ,"; and onward up to ten thousand: "We will bless the Lord our God, the God of Israel, the God of hosts, who sits between the Cherubim, for the food we have eaten . . ." (*Berakhot* 7:3). But this is a minor point. The main consideration is that God responds to the human will and expression of human intentionality. That becomes especially blatant when we turn to how God hears statements of what a human being wishes, or does not wish, joined to an act of consecration or sanctification through human words: vows, oaths, statements of sanctification and dedication, and the like. Here is where God's and the human person's encounter takes place—which is to say, at the human being's action and volition.

God hears not only prayers offered by the community but also vows and oaths taken by individuals. That is the foundation of the tractates on Vows (*Nedarim*), oaths (*Shabuot*), oaths of valuation of another person such as are specified at Leviticus 27:1ff. (*Arakhin*), and the special vow of the Nazirite (Numbers 6:1–21, tractate *Nazir*). To this list we may add numerous tractates that presuppose that God (directly or through angels or other messengers) confirms the stated intention of a human being. These include, for example, *Temurah*'s rules on designating gifts to the altar or to the upkeep of the Temple house, *Terumot*'s rules (representative of an equivalent premise governing tractates *Peah, Demai, Maaserot, Maaser Sheni, Hallah,* and *Bikkurim*) on the designation of a portion of the crop for God's share and use, and the like. The mere utterance of the appropriate words invokes, for the person who says them, a vow or an oath (depending on the formula, purpose, and occasion); such a statement then is binding and imposes concrete obligations of acts of commission or omission. A vow commonly compares a secular object to a holy one, such as imposing upon food the status of God's food upon the altar, and one who has imputed the sacred status to the food may not consume it. God then is assumed not only to have heard, but also to have taken account of the vow (or oath), an assumption that again implies immediacy and presence under all circumstances. God furthermore will take into account the attitude of mind or intentionality associated with a verbal expression, so there are vows that are not binding, such as those of incitement, exaggeration, error, and constraint (*Nedarim* 3:1). In such cases the statement is null; God knows the difference. The same principles in general apply to the special vow of the Nazirite.

Also it goes without saying that God knows not only public deeds, but also secret deeds. Consequently, God will settle the matter of a husband's jealousy of his wife by guiding the working of the bitter water in such a way as to show what, if anything, has actually taken place (Numbers 5:11–31, tractate *Sotah*). God's involvement in the rite is direct, since the name of God is written on the scroll prepared for the rite and then blotted out in the water that the woman has to drink. The oath that is imposed, of course, contains the expected implication that God hears oaths and punishes those taken in vain. In all of these aspects, God forms a powerful presence, if a systemically inert one, guaranteeing rules but not exhibiting distinctive traits. But the philosopher's conception of God competes in the Mishnah with yet another.

The authorship of the Tosefta, a supplement to the Mishnah, who flourished about a century after the completion of the Mishnah in ca. 200 C.E., presents materials of three kinds: (1) direct citation and gloss of the Mishnah's sentences; (2) exegesis, without direct citation, of the Mishnah's sentences, in discussions that are fully comprehensible only by reference to the Mishnah; and (3) statements that deal with the subject matter of the Mishnah but that are fully comprehensible without reference to the Mishnah. The first two types vastly predominate throughout the Tosefta's treatment of the Mishnah. The Tosefta appeals for order, structure, and program to the Mishnah's tractate. The Tosefta's pertinent materials do not vastly change the picture. The Presence of God, referred to by the word *Shekhinah,* makes an explicit appearance at Tosefta *Menahot* 7:8 with reference to the verse, "Moses saw all the work . . . and Moses blessed them" (Exodus 39:43): "With what blessing did he bless them? He said to them, 'May the Presence of God dwell with the work of your hands. . . .' " And further, "Just as you have been engaged in the work of making the tabernacle and the Presence of God has dwelled with the work of your hands, so may you have the merit of building before me the chosen house, and may the Presence of God dwell with the work of your hands." God's presence is furthermore acknowledged by the "you" of the liturgy, as in "May your will be done in heaven above, and grant ease to those that fear you" (Tosefta *Berakhot* 3:7, among numerous instances), so too, "May it be your will . . ." (Tosefta *Berakhot* 6:2, among many instances). God's presence (*Shekhinah*) is further said to depart from Israel because of the sin of murder (Tosefta *Yoma* 1:12; *Shebuot* 1:4) or for tale-bearing (Tosefta *Sotah* 14:3). The Presence waited upon various persons (Tosefta *Sotah* 4:7).

The confession for the Day of Atonement (Tosefta *Yoma* 2:1, 4:14) forms another occasion for acknowledging God's presence. Rules for reciting benedictions, such as in the Prayer, are spelled out also in the Tosefta (*Berakhot* 1:4ff.), with some to be marked by genuflection and others not. These rules again rest on the conviction that God is present when prayers are said. But the presence of God was not the sole consideration; the convenience of the community at large made a difference. By himself, Akiva would pray slowly and at length; with the community he cut matters (Tosefta *Berakhot* 3:5).

God as a person whom one might envisage and even see had formed the subject of interpretation of Ezekiel's vision of the Chariot (Ezekiel 1:4), but the framers of the Mishnah merely allude to that fact (*Hagigah* 2:1) and do not tell us the substance of the vision of God as a physical person. God's person, not merely presence, however, forms the presupposition of all acts of the recitation of prayer, which take for granted that God not only hears prayer but also cares what the human being requests. One example, among many, is the prayer of the high priest on the Day of Atonement: "O God, your people, the house of Israel, have committed iniquity, transgressed and sinned before you. O God, forgive the iniquities and transgressions and sins which your people, the house of Israel, have committed . . . as it is written in the Torah of your servant, Moses, 'For on this day shall atonement be made for you to clean you, from all your sins shall you be clean before the Lord (Leviticus 16:30)' " (Mishnah *Yoma* 6:2). God is everywhere a "you," and therefore a person.

Not only so, but, as a person, God is assumed to respond to words and events pretty much as human beings do. For example, when the community suffers from drought and prays for rain, not only is God asked to act as God had done in times past, "May the

one who answered our ancestors at the Red Sea answer you"
(Mishnah *Taanit* 2:4), but the acts of self-mortification and depri-
vation are meant to impress God and to win sympathy, much as
they would (it was assumed) from a mortal ruler.

Mishnah Taanit 2:1–4

The manner of fasting: how [was it done]?

They bring forth the ark into the street of the town and put wood ashes
on (1) the ark, (2) the head of the patriarch, and (3) the head of the court.

And each person puts ashes on his head.

The eldest among them makes a speech of admonition: "Our brothers,
concerning the people of Nineveh it is not said, 'And God saw their
sackcloth and their fasting,' but, And God saw their deeds, for they
repented from their evil way" (Jonah 3:10).

And in prophetic tradition it is said, "Rend your heart and not your
garments" (Joel 2:13).

They arise for prayer.

They bring down before the ark an experienced elder, who has children,
and whose cupboard [house] is empty, so that his heart should be wholly
in the prayer.

And he says before them twenty-four blessings:
the eighteen said every day, and he adds six more to them.

And these are:

(1) Remembrance verses, (2) Shofar verses, (3) In my distress I cried to
the Lord and he answered me (Psalms 120), (4) and, I will lift up my eyes
to the hills . . . (Psalms 121), (5) and, Out of the depths I have cried to
you, O Lord (Psalms 130), (6) and, A prayer of the afflicted when he is
overwhelmed (Psalms 102).

R. Judah says, "He did not have to say Remembrance verses and Shofar
verses. But in their stead he says, (1) If there be in the land famine, if there
be pestilence (1 Kings 8:37ff.). And, (2) The word of the Lord which came
to Jeremiah concerning the drought (Jeremiah 14:1ff.). And he concludes
each of them with its appropriate ending."

For the first [ending] he says, "He who answered Abraham on Mount
Moriah will answer you and hear the sound of your cry this day. Blessed
are you, O Lord, redeemer of Israel."

For the second he says, "He who answered our fathers at the Red Sea
will answer you and hear the sound of your cry this day. Blessed are you,
O Lord, who remembers forgotten things."

For the third he says, "He who answered Joshua at Gilgal will answer you and hear the sound of your cry this day. Blessed are you, O Lord, who hears the sound of the shofar."

For the fourth he says, "He who answered Samuel at Mispeh will answer you and hear the sound of your cry this day. Blessed are you, O Lord, who hears a cry."

For the fifth he says, "He who answered Elijah at Mount Carmel will answer you and hear the sound of your cry this day. Blessed are you, O Lord, who hears prayer."

For the sixth he says, "He who answered Jonah in the belly of the fish will answer you and hear the sound of your cry this day. Blessed are you, O Lord, who answers prayer in a time of trouble."

For the seventh he says, "He who answered David and Solomon, his son, in Jerusalem, will answer you and hear the sound of your cry this day. Blessed are you, O Lord, who has mercy on the Land."

The one who represents the community in prayer therefore was to be an elder, who had children for whom to worry and a house empty of food (Mishnah *Taanit* 2:2); such a one would then be wholehearted in the prayer. God would discern the sincerity and respond with sympathy. Hence God was understood as a person, in whose model the human being had been made, and human beings, searching their own hearts, could understand God's.

While, throughout the Mishnah we find the datum that God hears and answers prayer—for example, "When I enter [the house of study], I pray that no offense will take place on my account, and when I leave, I give thanks for my lot" (*Berakhot* 4:2)—that is not the end of the matter. Of still greater interest, God is assumed to take the form of a person, in the model of a heavenly monarch or emperor. For example, when one is reciting the Prayer, one is assumed to stand before the King, and that location, in God's presence, requires appropriate probity: "Even if the king greets a person, one is not to reply, and even if a snake wrapped itself around one's heel, one is not to interrupt" (*Berakhot* 5:1). The response to the recitation of prayer derives not from concrete personal engagement by God; there is no story in the Mishnah that suggests anyone believed God talked back to the one who says the prayer. But there are explicit statements that God heard and answered prayer and so indicated on the spot:

Berakhot 5:5

If one who recites the Prayer makes an error, it is a bad omen for that person, and if that person recited the Prayer in behalf of the entire community, it is a bad omen for those who assigned the task to that person. . . .

They said of R. Hanina b. Dosa "When he would pray for the sick, he would say, "This one shall live," or, "That one shall die."

They said to him, "How do you know?"

He said to them, "If my prayer flows easily in my mouth, I know that it is accepted, [and the person will live]. "But if not I know that it is rejected [and the person will die]."

God as "you" occurs not only in liturgy, but also in legal formulas recited upon specified occasions. Here, to be sure, the language, as much as the context, is defined by Scripture:

Maaser Sheni 5:10–13

". . . I have removed . . . according to all your commandment which you have commanded me . . ." [Deuteronomy 26:13ff.]. . . .

"Look down from your holy habitation from heaven:" We have done what you have decreed concerning us, now you do what you have promised to us. . . .

The transaction is between two persons, each bound by the same rule as governs the other.

But the person-hood of God as a "you" plays a role principally in the address of prayer. Scripture's portrait of God as an active personality finds no counterpart whatsoever in the Mishnah. That fact may be seen in a simple observation. The majestic presence of God in the unfolding of events, which forms the great theme of the scriptural narratives of ancient Israel's history, may define a premise of the Mishnah's worldview. But at no passage in the Mishnah does an action of God serve to explain an event, nor do we find lessons drawn, from events, as to God's purpose or will. Events take place, truths endure, but the two form a merely assumed and implicit relationship. In passages in which important events are catalogued, for example, God's action is not at issue. Interestingly, these events are always catalogued as completed actions and in the past tense, changes of circumstance or situation, not decisions and actions of a divine monarch deciding from day to day what is to be done and then doing it:

Mishnah Sotah 9:12–15

When the first prophets died, Urim and Thummim ceased. When the Temple was destroyed, the Shamir-worm ceased . . . and faithful men came to an end, as it is written, "Help, Lord, for the godly man ceases" (Psalms 12:2). . . . During the war of Vespasian, they forbade the crowns of the bridegrooms and the wedding drum. During the war of Titus, they forbade the crowns of the brides and that a man should teach his son Greek. In the last war they forbade the bride to go forth in a palanquin inside the city. . . . When R. Meir died, there were no more makers of parables. . . .

Along these same lines, when at Mishnah *Zebahim* 14:4–8, diverse periods in the history of the cult are specified, we find no invocation of the action or purpose of God. That is not to suggest that anyone imagined God had not done these things by decree. It is only to point out that the sorts of explicit conclusions drawn from historical events by the prophetic historians in Joshua, Judges, Samuel, and Kings, for example, find no counterpart in the Mishnah. God now *presides* as much as in the biblical narratives God truly ruled, but the appeal is particular to the Mishnah:

Mishnah Sotah 9:9–16

When murderers became many, the rite of breaking the heifer's neck was cancelled.

[This was] when Eleazar b. Dinai came along, and he was also called Tehinah b. Perishah. Then they called him, "Son of a murderer."

When adulterers became many, the ordeal of the bitter water was cancelled.

And Rabban Yohanan b. Zakkai cancelled it, since it is said, "I will not punish your daughters when they commit whoredom, nor your daughters-in-law when they commit adultery, for they themselves go apart with whores" (Hosea 4:14).

When Yose b. Yoezer of Seredah and Yose b. Yohanan of Jerusalem died, the grape clusters were cancelled, since it is said, "There is no cluster to eat, my soul desires the first ripe fig" (Micah 7:1).

Yohanan, high priest, did away with the confession concerning tithe.

Also: He cancelled the rite of the Awakeners and the Stunners,

Until his time a hammer did strike in Jerusalem.

And in his time no man had to ask concerning doubtfully tithed produce.

When the Sanhedrin was cancelled, singing at wedding feasts was cancelled, since it is said, "They shall not drink wine with a song" (Isaiah 24:9).

When the former prophets died out, the Urim and Tummim were cancelled.

When the sanctuary was destroyed, the Shamir worm ceased and [so did] the honey of supim.

And faithful men came to an end, since it is written, "Help, O Lord, for the godly man ceases" (Psalms 12:2).

Rabban Simeon b. Gamaliel says in the name of R. Joshua, "From the day on which the Temple was destroyed, there is no day on which there is no curse, and dew has not come down as a blessing. The good taste of produce is gone."

R. Yose says, "Also: the fatness of produce is gone."

R. Simeon b. Eleazar says,"[When] purity [ceased], it took away the taste and scent; [when] tithes [ceased], they took away the fatness of corn."

And sages say, "Fornication and witchcraft made an end to everything."

In the war against Vespasian they decreed against the wearing of wreaths by bridegrooms and against the wedding drum.

In the war against Titus they decreed against the wearing of wreaths by brides,

And [they decreed] that a man should not teach Greek to his son.

In the last war [Bar Kokhba's] they decreed that a bride should not go out in a palanquin inside the town.

But our rabbis [thereafter] permitted the bride to go out in a palanquin inside the town.

When R. Meir died, makers of parables came to an end.

When Ben Azzai died, diligent students came to an end.

When Ben Zoma died, exegetes came to an end.

When R. Joshua died, goodness went away from the world.

When Rabban Simeon b. Gamaliel died, the locust came, and troubles multiplied.

When R. Eleazar b. Azariah died, wealth went away from the sages.

When R. Akiva died, the glory of the Torah came to an end.

When R. Hanina b. Dosa died, wonder workers came to an end.

When R. Yose Qatnuta died, pietists went away.

(And why was he called Qatnuta? Because he was the least of the pietists.)

When Rabban Yohanan b. Zakkai died, the splendor of wisdom came to an end.

When Rabban Gamaliel the Elder died, the glory of the Torah came to an end, and cleanness and separateness perished.

When R. Ishmael b. Phabi died, the splendor of the priesthood came to an end.

When Rabbi died, modesty and fear of sin came to an end.

R. Pinhas b. Yair says, "When the Temple was destroyed, associates became ashamed and so did free men, and they covered their heads.

"And wonder workers became feeble. And violent men and big talkers grew strong.

"And none expounds and none seeks [learning] and none asks.

"Upon whom shall we depend? Upon our Father in heaven."

R. Eliezer the Great says, "From the day on which the Temple was destroyed, sages began to be like scribes, and scribes like ministers, and ministers like ordinary folk.

"And the ordinary folk have become feeble.

"And none seeks.

"Upon whom shall we depend? Upon our Father in heaven."

With the footprints of the Messiah: presumption increases, and the vine gives its fruit and wine at great cost.

And the government turns to heresy

And there is no reproof, and dearth increases.

The gathering place will be for prostitution.

And Galilee will be laid waste.

And the Gablan will be made desolate.

And the men of the frontier will go about from town to town, and none will take pity on them.

And the wisdom of scribes will putrefy.

And those who fear sin will be rejected.

And the truth will be locked away.

Children will shame elders, and elders will stand up before children.

For the son dishonors the father and the daughter rises up against her mother, the daughter-in-law against her mother-in-law; a man's enemies are the men of his own house (Micah 7:6).

The face of the generation in the face of a dog.

A son is not ashamed before his father.

Upon whom shall we depend? Upon our Father in heaven.

R. Pinhas b. Yair says, "Heedfulness leads to cleanliness, cleanliness leads to cleanness, cleanness leads to abstinence, abstinence leads to holiness, holiness leads to modesty, modesty leads to the fear of sin, the fear of sin leads to piety, piety leads to the Holy Spirit, the Holy Spirit leads to the resurrection of the dead, and the resurrection of the dead comes through Elijah, blessed be his memory, Amen."

R. Phineas b. Yair said, "When the Temple was destroyed, . . . men of violence and loud tongue prevailed. No one expounds, no one seeks, no one asks. On whom may we rely? On our father in heaven. . . ."

R. Eliezer the elder says, "Since the temple was destroyed, sages diminished to the standing of school teachers, school teachers to synagogue beadles, synagogue beadles to people of no standing . . . , and none was there to seek. On whom may we rely? On our father in heaven. . . ."

The contrary picture, of course, makes its mark: "With the footprints of the Messiah presumptions shall increase . . ." (*Sotah* 9:16), once more language noteworthy for its failure to speak directly and immediately of God's intervention. The plan prevails, the person plays no explicit part. Once more, God forms a premise, scarcely a person, in the unfolding of vast events of politics and history. That fact sets the stage for the most important observation, which is, in the nature of things, a negative one.

In the Tosefta's amplification of the Mishnah, God's communication with biblical figures is of course noted. God spoke with Moses, Abraham, Jacob, Samuel, and others (Tosefta *Berakhot* 12ff.), but these passages take for granted merely the facts of the biblical narrative. God's attitudes compare to those of mortals: "One in whom people take delight, God takes delight" (*Berakhot* 3:3). God is a person with emotions such as anger and mercy, so: If when God is angry at the righteous, he has mercy on them, when he is disposed to be merciful, how much more does he have mercy on them! (*Berakhot* 4:16). God respects learning, of course, and is affronted when religious duties are carried out in an ignorant way (*Berakhot* 6:18). The saying of Hillel which follows can be read as a statement imputed to God: "If you will come to my house, I shall come to your house. If you will not come to my house, I shall not come to your house, as it is said, 'In every place where I cause my name to be remembered I will come to you and bless you'" (Exodus 20:21) (Tosefta *Sukkah* 4:3). If so, God is saying that those who come to the Temple will receive God in their houses, a clear indication of God as person, not merely premise or even presence.

God does not approve arrogance and favors the humble, a point repeatedly made in a review of the ancient history of creation: "The generation of the Flood acted arrogantly before the Omnipresent only on account of the good which he lavished on them . . . that is what caused them to say to God . . . The Omnipresent said to them, 'By the goodness which I lavished on them do they take pride before me? By that same good I shall exact punishment from them'" (Tosefta *Sotah* 3:6–8, and so for the men of the Tower, Sodom, Egyptians, Samson, Absalom, Sennacherib, Nebuchadnezzar (*Sotah* 3:9–19). The statement attributed to God is not representative of a conversation of a vivid personality; rather it is an observation of a merely theological character, that is, the rendering in conversation form of a principle that God exacts punishment for arrogance and ingratitude, and does so through that very matter that brings up the arrogance or ingratitude. The contrary position—that God also responds to what the patriarchs and matriarchs and other saints did by favoring the descendants—is clearly spelled out as well: for example: Abraham went and got a morsel of bread for the angels (Genesis 18:5), so God gave manna in the wilderness (Numbers 11:8), and so on as a counterpart construction (Tosefta *Sotah* 4:1–19). The same principle of divine reciprocity is expressed in connection with Deuteronomy 26:17–18, "You have declared this day concerning the Lord that he is your God." So, the passage goes on, "Said the Holy One . . . to them, 'Just as you have made me the only object of your love in the world, so I shall make you the only object of my love in the world to come'" (*Sotah* 7:10). This propositional statement does not convey the characterization of the one who said it, for instance expressing the personal traits of God. It simply states, in yet another way, the basic thesis of Tosefta *Sotah* throughout, which is the prevalence of the principle of measure for measure in the fate of Israel. So too when there is heavenly communication in both the Mishnah and the Tosefta, it is ordinarily through the medium of a heavenly echo (e.g., Tosefta *Sotah* 13:5ff.). God of course exacts punishment from the wicked and rewards the righteous (e.g., Tosefta *Sanhedrin* 8:3).

If God is conceived as not merely a person but possessed of specific traits of personality, the Mishnah hardly contains evidence that its authorship could specify what those personal traits might be. True enough, one may infer from the rules that the Mishnah contains the attitudes of mind and preferences of personality of the God as premise, who even is invoked as presence. For instance, God is assumed to favor deeds of lovingkindness and study of the Torah; honoring of parents; making peace among people. Accordingly, God may be assumed, as a personality, to be generous, studious, respectful, and irenic, a picture explicitly limned in tractate *Avot*. But no *stories* in particular portray God in one way rather than in some other. No other modes of discourse, beside stories, portray God as a distinct personality who in some vivid and concrete way embodies the desired virtues. God is not portrayed as walking, talking, caring, acting as people do. Once more, only when we do examine such explicit portraits of the incarnation of God shall we understand the remarkable reticence of the Mishnah on this matter.

True, we may impute such traits and others to the God that serves as premise and even presence. But the authorship of the Mishnah, unlike the diverse scriptural writers, simply did not portray God as a personality. Nor, apart from liturgical settings, is its fixed premise of God as giver of the Torah translated into the notion of the active presence of God in the here and now. God hears and answers prayers of the individual—setting aside the general rules of being when God chooses to do so. The way in which an authorship among the canonical documents of the Judaism of the Dual Torah does portray the personality of God will show us, in due course, a drastic shift in the modes of discourse concerning God.

In only one story in the entire Mishnah do I find a hint that God has a personality and therefore approaches the condition of incarnation in some concrete setting. Specifically, there is imputed to God a rather wry sense of humor, but the matter appears with remarkable subtlety. It is in the account of how Honi, the circle drawer, in a rather childish way required God to give rain:

Mishnah Taanit 3:8

On account of every sort of public trouble (may it not happen) do they sound the shofar, except for an excess of rain.

They said to Honi, the circle drawer, "Pray for rain."

He said to them, "Go and take in the clay ovens used for Passover, so that they not soften [in the rain which is coming]."

He prayed, but it did not rain.

What did he do?

He drew a circle and stood in the middle of it and said before Him, "Lord of the world! Your children have turned to me, for before you I am like a member of the family. I swear by your great name—I'm simply not moving from here until you take pity on your children!"

It began to rain drop by drop.

He said, "This is not what I wanted, but rain for filling up cisterns, pits, and caverns."

It began to rain violently.

He said, "This is not what I wanted, but rain of good will, blessing, and graciousness."

Now it rained the right way, until Israelites had to flee from Jerusalem up to the Temple Mount because of the rain.

Now they came and said to him, "Just as you prayed for it to rain, now pray for it to go away."

He said to them, "Go, see whether the stone of the strayers is disappeared."

Simeon b. Shetah said to him, "If you were not Honi, I should decree a ban of excommunication against you. But what am I going to do to you? For you importune before the Omnipresent, so he does what you want, like a son who importunes his father, so he does what he wants. Concerning you Scripture says, Let your father and your mother be glad, and let her that bore you rejoice (Proverbs 23:25)."

The picture in this very funny story of a rather petulant God, giving what was asked in such a way as to make fun of Honi, draws us near to a God with an interesting personality, no longer defined only by traits framed as rules, such as merciful and just, but now characterized as acting as the occasion required. Narrative in general finds more than slight place in the Mishnah, since the entire account of the Temple and its cult, the rites of the altar, the priesthood and their activities, is presented in essentially narrative form. But narrative never serves in the Mishnah as a vehicle for discussing the personality or activity of God.

Indeed, even when the opportunity to do so presents itself, the authorship of the Mishnah does not respond. The occasions that in Scripture commonly provoke God's anger—hence portraying God's personality in concrete terms—involve idolatry, generating God's jealousy. The counterpart discourse in the Mishnah deals with worship of alien gods in *Abodah Zarah*. No passage in that tractate refers to God's anger or jealousy when Israelites worship idols. It is simply not a component of the discourse. In the Mishnah's treatment, what is at stake is the relationship between Israelites and Gentiles, not between Israel and God, and the purpose of the law is to define permissible and impermissible transactions with Gentiles upon their celebration of their idol-gods. Secondary issues, such as use of foods prepared by Gentiles, disposition of pieces of idols, and the like, do not change the picture of an authorship interested in outlining the boundaries between holy Israel and the Gentile world. A simple fact remains to be noted. As in the Mishnah, so in the Tosefta, we find not a single story in which God is represented as a vivid personality.

The authorship of the Mishnah, like Israel in general, lived in a social world in which God formed a formidable presence everywhere. No wonder there was no necessity constantly to restate the premise of God's rule and authority. Quite to the contrary, in the course of setting forth the law, only a few tractates explicitly refer to God, and most do not. The former classification of tractates, such as *Berakhot* and *Taanit*, involve liturgy, and the bulk of the explicit allusions to God, whether as premise or as person, appear quite naturally in discussion of prayer, with special attention to where, when, why, and above all, how one says prayers (including blessings, supplications, thanksgiving, and the like). The latter tractates—nearly the whole of the Mishnah—implicitly refer to God in relation to such topics as the proper conduct of rites on the appointed seasons, the correct procedures of the sacrificial cult, the maintenance of the priesthood and the Temple, and the protection of the Temple from contamination.

Accordingly, when we wish to hear how the Mishnah's authorship speaks of the premise of God's rule and presence, we may point for systematic statements of an implicit character to the divisions of *Agriculture* (maintaining the priesthood, giving God the share of the crop that is due to the divinity), *Appointed Seasons* (laws governing conduct on holy occasions such as the Sabbath and festivals), *Holy Things* (rules for the conduct of the everyday rites of the Temple and for the upkeep of the building), and *Purities* (laws on uncleanness, to begin with those affecting the cult, as is specified in the book of Leviticus). We may further discover in the division of *Women,* which governs family life, a systematic expression of God's acute interest in the sanctification of a woman's sexuality to a particular man, such that under some conditions sexual activity is punishable by Heaven, while under others that same activity enjoys Heaven's approval and blessing. Here, too, in the exposition of the requirements of sanctification of the woman and sanctity of the family, I find implicit the premise of God's governance. Only the division of *Damages* fails to offer quite direct testimony to the same proposition, and even here we may find numerous specific statements, as in *Sanhedrin* 10:1ff., on the requirement, if one wishes to be (an) "Israel," of confessing that the resurrection of the dead constitutes a scripturally ordained truth. Statements of that order point toward the prevailing premise, and permit us to claim quite simply that God as systemic premise is never far from the surface of the law of the Mishnah and is, commonly, quite visible to the naked eye.

But that fact raises more questions than it settles, for it leads us to wonder how active a part God plays in the system of the Mishnah. Can that system have taken shape without the premise of God? Certainly not. Does that system, however, appeal to God, whether premise, whether presence, in the pursuit of solutions to its problems? Certainly not. And the exceptions to the rule are not only few but readily explained within the rules of the system, so hardly present exceptions at all. The focus of that system is on the discovery of the rules that govern a given classification of items—objects, facts, events—and (mostly in the secondary and exegetical work generated by the Mishnah) the harmonization of the prevailing rules with one another. The authorship of the Mishnah assigns to God, through the Torah, both priority and also a position of essential passivity, as a well-crafted legal system requires. For a

God who intervenes violates the law, and, to the philosophers of the Mishnah, God guarantees the truth and regularity of the laws, deriving as they do from the Torah, but in particular cases God does not enforce those laws, nor should God have to. The very nature of the system prevents it. Allowing God under specified circumstances to hear and answer prayer need not, and does not, violate the orderly nature of the system, since the circumstances can be specified and the required conditions met. So, in all, the emphasis on rules leaves God as mere premise, not as active force in the system of the Mishnah.

Shall we then compare God to the laws of gravity? Once we recognize that God defines a ubiquitous premise but never an independent variable, we see the aptness of such a metaphor. The laws of gravity, to a systematic account of the ecology of a botanical world, constitute a given and immutable fact. Without those laws, grass cannot sprout and trees cannot grow in the way in which they now do. But the laws of gravity, while necessary, are hardly sufficient—or, once conceded, even very urgent. They do not dictate many important systemic facts (though they make possible all facts) and they do not settle many of the system's interesting questions. So the laws of gravity in botany prove at once necessary and insufficient for explanation—implicit and ubiquitous, but not at all generative. Indeed, when we ask about the importance of the laws of gravity in a theory of botany (or biology, or plate-tectonics in geology), we see how awry matters have become. The laws are absolutely necessary but, even when sufficient, still not very interesting. And, to come to the worldview before us, we are therefore constrained to ask ourselves: Where is the God who acts? Where is the God who cares? Where is the God who rules "Israel" in accord with the Torah? In this system of philosophers with its law-abiding, philosophically acceptable God, the answer is, no-where. Later on, in a system dependent upon the Mishnah's, God would become not only necessary but also sufficient. But while without God the authorship of the Mishnah cannot have constructed their system, to which God is necessary, still, since that authorship could frame all of the system's most compelling propositions without God, God was hardly sufficient for the explanation of the system. God in the Mishnah's system is everywhere present, the ground of all being, giver and guarantor of the Torah—and a monumental irrelevance.

True, in any account of the Judaism "out there," beyond the pages of the Mishnah and yet presupposed and confessed by the authorship of the Mishnah, we must begin with God. Certainly the worldview of the Mishnah takes shape around the datum of God's creation of the world and giving of the Torah. No one can imagine otherwise. But then that Judaism "out there" scarcely intersects with the profound concerns and urgent questions of the Judaism "in here," that is, in the system of the Mishnah in particular. The Judaism "out there" turns out to make very little difference in the shaping and direction of the Judaism "in here," in the formation and structure of the worldview of the system at hand, and to contribute no more than the system builders can utilize—if also no less.

3

God's Presence in the Torah: Meeting God in Mind, Imagination, and Emotion

F rom the Mishnah, we come to its first and most important introduction, which is tractate *Avot,* a compilation that was concluded in ca. 250, about a half-century after the Mishnah. Its authorship strings together sayings of important authorities, from Sinai to one generation beyond the redaction of the Mishnah itself. The composition, called in English "the sayings of the fathers," quite naturally rests upon the premises of the document it explains, but precisely how God appears in *Avot* is not to be predicted merely on that basis. The tractate is both brief and critical to the entire statement of the Judaism of the Dual Torah, and the first four chapters are here reviewed.

It was at prayer that the authorship of tractate *Avot* encountered God as person, not merely as premise or even as presence. Still more generally, God as person cared for the sources of human action and understood proper from improper motivation. But what God does not do in the tractate is play an active part in the everyday encounter of sages and Heaven. By that I mean that these sages did not report on God's discourse with them, what God said to them and what they said to God; they did not tell stories about God's doings.

True, they took for granted that God spoke to the prophets and that the Torah contained God's word. They do not, however, represent conversations between human and divine personalities, and they do not—at this stage in the unfolding of the canon—record encounters between God as an active personality and a human being, presumably a sage. Only when we have surveyed documents that do record God's conversations with sages and resort to sustained narratives to portray God's dealings with people shall we have a clear picture of what it means to render God as a fully incarnate personality. At that point we shall see also why it is necessary to resort to a mode of discourse not present in our tractate, specifically to narrative and, within narrative, storytelling. When God is premise, presence, and even (implicit) person, sayings suffice, for we make reference to a premise, allude to a presence, and respond to a person. When it comes to portraying a fully vital personality, by contrast, for the authorships at hand (and, I am inclined to think, for all authorships) the incarnate God requires narrative, especially story, for a full portrait. That God will make a full appearance in the Judaism of the Dual Torah. But not yet.

Chapter 1

Moses received the Torah at Sinai and handed it on to Joshua, Joshua to elders, and elders to prophets. And prophets handed it on to the men of the great assembly. They said three things: "Be prudent in judgment. Raise up many disciples. Make a fence for the Torah."

The Mishnah's great apologia begins with remarkable reticence about the source of the Torah, but of course the authorship takes for granted that God gave what Moses received. Then why not say so? The obvious answer is that the point important for this authorship was not the source but the mode of transmission and what was handed on, which was the Torah, and that is what is at stake in the allegation contained in the chain of tradition. God constitutes precisely what, in the Mishnah, we anticipate: the premise.

From this point onward, where God forms a presence, it will be by inference, with reference to "Heaven," and through similar circumlocutions and circumventions of the obvious. The presence of God makes a difference to one's attitude or intention; one relates to God through right attitude, which is one of acceptance and loyal service, rather than in an exchange between equals, let alone coercion. In what follows, God or "Heaven" defines right attitudes.

Simeon the Righteous was one of the last survivors of the great assembly. He would say: "On three things does the world stand: On the Torah, and on the Temple service, and on deeds of lovingkindness."

Antigonus of Sokho received [the Torah] from Simeon the Righteous. He would say: "Do not be like servants who serve the master on condition of receiving a reward, but [be] like servants who serve the master not on condition of receiving a reward. And let the fear of Heaven be upon you."

The correct attitude toward God is awe, "fear of heaven" expressing that right attitude. At this point we find in an explicit statement the issue of intentionality (the reason one does the right thing) joined with the relationship to God. One should serve God with the correct intention, which is awe or fear, not as an act of condescension or choice but as one of obligation and duty. Here we find the missing link between intentionality and God, and at this point the Mishnaic system takes within its active and generative framework what in the Mishnah itself seemed to me remote. God then is present and, further, as person, also responds to and cares about the human person's attitude. God is not merely the one who gave the Torah, that is, who made the rules. God is now the one who, day to day and everywhere, sees to the correct working of the rules. And God knows and responds to the attitudes of those who obey the rules, hence, is a person. The proportion and place of God in the spinning out of the sayings should not, however, be overestimated, as the following long string of sayings of a juridical character indicates.

Yosé ben Yoezer of Zeredah and Yosé ben Yohanan of Jerusalem received [the Torah] from them. Yosé ben Yoezer says: "Let your house be a gathering place for sages. And wallow in the dust of their feet, and drink in their words with gusto."

Yosé ben Yohanan of Jerusalem says: "Let your house be open wide. And seat the poor at your table ['make the poor members of your household']. And don't talk too much with women." (He referred to a man's wife, all the more so is the rule to be applied to the wife of one's fellow. In this regard did sages say: "So long as a man talks too much with a woman, he brings trouble on himself, wastes time better spent on studying the Torah, and ends up an heir of Gehenna.")

Joshua ben Perahyah and Nittai the Arbelite received [the Torah] from them. Joshua ben Perahyah says: "Set up a master for yourself. And get yourself a companion-disciple. And give everybody the benefit of the doubt."

Nittai the Arbelite says: "Keep away from a bad neighbor. And don't get involved with a bad person. And don't give up hope of retribution."

Judah ben Tabbai and Simeon ben Shetah received [the Torah] from them.

Judah ben Tabbai says: "Don't make yourself like one of those who advocate before judges [while you yourself are judging a case]. And when the litigants stand before you, regard them as guilty. But when they leave you, regard them as acquitted (when they have accepted your judgment)."

Simeon ben Shetah says: "Examine the witnesses with great care. And watch what you say, lest they learn from what you say how to lie."

Shemaiah and Avtalyon received [the Torah] from them. Shemaiah says: "Love work. Hate authority. Don't get friendly with the government."

Avtalyon says: "Sages, watch what you say, lest you become liable to the punishment of exile, and go into exile to a place of bad water, and disciples who follow you drink bad water and die, and the name of Heaven be thereby profaned."

Once more the entry of Heaven carries in its wake instructions on correct motivation or attitude. One should follow the stated rule so as to avoid disgracing Heaven. Then along with an attitude of service and obligation comes the sanction of fear of shame. God the person shares the attitudes of humanity, being anthropopathic or congruent in feelings and emotions. That premise, present now, runs through the document. It will not have surprised the authorship of the Mishnah, with its keen interest in attitude and conduct when one is at prayer, in the assumption that God pays attention to such matters, as would an earthly ruler.

Hillel and Shammai received [the Torah] from them. Hillel says: "Be disciples of Aaron, loving peace and pursuing grace, loving people and drawing them near to the Torah."

He would say [in Aramaic]: "A name made great is a name destroyed, and one who does not add, subtracts.

And who does not learn is liable to death. And the one who uses the crown, passes away."

He would say: "If I am not for myself, who is for me? And when I am for myself, what am I? And if not now, when?"

Shammai says: "Make your learning of the Torah a fixed obligation. Say little and do much. Greet everybody cheerfully."

Rabban Gamaliel says: "Set up a master for yourself. Avoid doubt. Don't tithe by too much guesswork."

Simeon his son says: "All my life I grew up among the sages, and I found nothing better for a person [the body] than silence. And not the learning is the thing, but the doing. And whoever talks too much causes sin."

Rabban Simeon ben Gamaliel says: "On three things does the world stand: on justice, on truth, and on peace. As it is said, 'Execute the judgment of truth and peace in your gates' (Zechariah 8:16)."

The opening chain of tradition twice makes the same important point concerning the right attitude toward heaven. God assuredly forms the implicit premise of the account of the origin and transmission of the Torah. Yet if we were to ask where and how God plays a part as fully exposed personality, I cannot point to a pertinent passage. God as presence and person comes to ample instantiation here. But that reaches the limits of metaphor: God is like a human being in feeling and attitude. Nothing in tractate *Avot* Chapters 2, 3, and 4 changes that picture or augments it. Still, surveying the text will allow the reader to examine the way in which the Mishnah's great apologists have set forth, in their own words, the character of divinity as they wish to portray that character.

Chapter 2

Rabbi says: "What is the straight path which a person should choose for himself? Whatever is an ornament to the one who follows it, and an ornament in the view of others. Be meticulous in a small religious duty as in a large one, for you do not know what sort of reward is coming for any of the various religious duties. And reckon with the loss [required] in carrying out a religious duty against the reward for doing it; and the reward for committing a transgression against the loss for doing it. And keep your eye on three things, so you will not come into the clutches of transgression. Know what is above you: An eye which sees, and an ear which hears, and all your actions are written down in a book."

The eye which sees, the ear which hears, the book—these now constitute a presence, which, in the nature of things, we are justified in naming God. God then hears and knows all things that individuals do, a position that accords with the Mishnah's view that God hears and answers prayer and responds to appropriate petition.

Rabban Gamaliel, a son of Rabbi Judah the Patriarch says: "Fitting is learning in the Torah along with a craft, for the labor put into the two of them makes one forget sin. And all learning of the Torah which is not joined with labor is destined to be null and causes sin. And all who work with the community—let them work with them [the community] for the sake of Heaven. For the merit of the fathers strengthens them, and the righteousness which they do stands forever. And, as for you, I credit you with a great reward, as if you had done [all the work required by the community]."

"For the sake of Heaven," that is, "for God's sake," defines the correct intention or motive. What that means is pretty much coherent with the earlier appeal, namely, for the service of God, not for one's own benefit.

"Be wary of the government, for they get friendly with a person only for their own convenience. They look like friends when it is to their benefit, but they do not stand by a person when he is in need."

He would say: "Make His wishes into your own wishes, so that He will make your wishes into His wishes. Put aside your wishes on account of His wishes, so that He will put aside the wishes of other people in favor of your wishes." Hillel says: "Do not walk out on the community. And do not have confidence in yourself until the day you die. And do not judge your companion until you are in his place. And do not say anything which cannot be heard, for in the end it will be heard. And do not say: 'When I have time, I shall study,' for you may never have time."

Serving "for the sake of Heaven" finds its counterpart in another statement on right attitude. One should want what God wants, so that God will want what the person wants. This is immediately qualified: one should accede to God's wishes over one's own desires, which will provoke a counterpart action in Heaven. Here God finds representation as, if not a personality, then a person, with wishes that respond to those of the human being. I cannot point in the Mishnah to an explicit statement of that view, though God's confirmation of human intention forms a persistent motif in the articulation of the Mishnah's law. What is therefore striking is the certainty of the authorship before us that God's feelings and emotions and desires correspond to those of humanity. One's duty, then, is to subordinate one's feelings and desires to those of God, conceived once more as the master to whom everyone relates as subordinate—but who then will respond to the will and wishes of subordinates of appropriate demeanor and conduct.

He would say: "A coarse person will never fear sin, nor will an *am ha aretz* ever be pious, nor will a shy person learn, nor will an ignorant person teach, nor will anyone too occupied in business get wise. In a place where there are no individuals, try to be an individual."

Also, he saw a skull floating on the water and said to it [in Aramaic]: "Because you drowned others, they drowned you, and in the end those who drowned you will be drowned."

Here is a routine allegation about the perfect justice meted out from Heaven. This has no bearing on God as person, but it does presuppose God's constant overseeing of earthly transactions and the divine interest in a just and fair settlement of all debts.

He would say: "Lots of meat, lots of worms; lots of property, lots of worries; lots of women, lots of witchcraft; lots of slave girls, lots of lust; lots of slave boys, lots of robbery. Lots of the Torah, lots of life; lots of discipleship, lots of wisdom; lots of counsel, lots of understanding; lots of righteousness, lots of peace. [If] one has gotten a good name, he has gotten it for himself. [If] he has gotten teachings of the Torah, he has gotten himself life eternal."

The notion of Torah teachings as guarantor of eternal life rests on the premise of God as giver of the Torah.

Rabban Yohanan ben Zakkai received [the Torah] from Hillel and Shammai. He would say: "If you have learned much Torah, do not puff yourself up on that account, for it was for that purpose that you were created." He had five disciples, and these are they: Rabbi Eliezer ben Hyrcanus, Rabbi Joshua ben Hananiah, Rabbi Yosé the Priest, Rabbi Simeon ben Nethanel, and Rabbi Eleazar ben Arakh.

He would list their good qualities: Rabbi Eliezer ben Hyrcanus—a plastered well, which does not lose a drop of water. Rabbi Joshua—happy is the one who gave birth to him. Rabbi Yosé—a pious man. Rabbi Simeon ben Nethanel—a man who fears sin. And Rabbi Eleazar ben Arakh—a surging spring.

He would say: "If all the sages of Israel were on one side of the scale, and Rabbi Eliezer ben Hyrcanus were on the other, he would outweigh all of them."

Abba Saul says in his name: "If all the sages of Israel were on one side of the scale, and Rabbi Eliezer ben Hyrcanus was also with them, and Rabbi Eleazar [ben Arakh] were on the other side, he would outweigh all of them."

He said to them: "Go and see what is the straight path to which someone should stick."

Rabbi Eliezer says: "A generous spirit." Rabbi Joshua says: "A good friend." Rabbi Yosé says: "A good neighbor." Rabbi Simeon says: "Foresight." Rabbi Eleazar says: "Good will."

He said to them: "I prefer the opinion of Rabbi Eleazar ben Arakh, because in what he says is included everything you say."

He said to them: "Go out and see what is the bad road, which someone should avoid." Rabbi Eliezer says: "Envy." Rabbi Joshua says: "A bad friend." Rabbi Yosé says: "A bad neighbor." Rabbi Simeon says: "A loan." (All the same is a loan owed to a human being and a loan owed to the Omnipresent, the blessed, as it is said, "The wicked borrows and does not pay back, but the righteous person deals graciously and hands over [what is owed])" (Psalms 37:21.)

Rabbi Eleazar says: "Ill will."

He said to them: "I prefer the opinion of Rabbi Eleazar ben Arakh, because in what he says is included everything you say."

They [each] said three things.

Rabbi Eliezer says: "Let the respect owing to your companion be as precious to you as the respect owing to yourself. And don't be easy to anger. And repent one day before you die. And warm yourself by the fire of the sages, but be careful of their coals, so you don't get burned—for their bite is the bite of a fox, and their sting is the sting of a scorpion, and their hiss is like the hiss of a snake, and everything they say is like fiery coals."

Rabbi Joshua says: "Envy, desire of bad things, and hatred for people push a person out of the world."

Rabbi Yosé says: "Let your companion's money be as precious to you as your own. And get yourself ready to learn the Torah, for it does not come as an inheritance to you. And may everything you do be for the sake of Heaven."

Rabbi Simeon says: "Be meticulous about the recitation of the Shema and the Prayer. And when you pray, don't treat your praying as a matter of routine; but let it be a [plea for] mercy and supplication before the

Omnipresent, the blessed, as it is said, 'For He is gracious and full of compassion, slow to anger and full of mercy, and repents of the evil' (Joel 2:13). And never be evil in your own eyes.''

The authorship of the Mishnah's rules about right attitude in prayer—correct intentionality, for instance—will not have found these statements surprising. The imputation to God of the traits of heart and attitude set forth by the prophet seems to me of secondary importance.

Rabbi Eleazar says: "Be constant in learning of the Torah; And know what to reply to an Epicurean; And know before whom you work, for your employer can be depended upon to pay your wages for what you do."

Rabbi Tarfon says: "The day is short, the work formidable, the workers lazy, the wages high, the employer impatient."

He would say: "It's not your job to finish the work, but you are not free to walk away from it. If you have learned much Torah, they will give you a good reward. And your employer can be depended upon to pay your wages for what you do. And know what sort of reward is going to be given to the righteous in the coming time."

These sayings are consistent with those in the opening chapter about the right attitude toward God. One should be the faithful slave, who performs in good conscience and with good will, out of duty, above all, out of trust that God will be present to pay a valid reward for what one does.

Chapter 3

Aqabiah b. Mehallalel says, "Reflect upon three things and you will not fall into the clutches of transgression: Know from whence you come, whither you are going, and before whom you are going to have to give a full account of yourself.

"From whence do you come? From a putrid drop. Whither are you going? To a place of dust, worms, and maggots.

"And before whom are you going to give a full account of yourself? Before the King of kings of kings, the Holy One, blessed be he.''

We come from nowhere, we go to death, we give our account before the heavenly King, God on high. The familiar attitude that before God as person one gives a full account will have found a ready hearing among the authors of the Mishnah. The important thing is once more the linking of God as person to the correct attitude toward God as person. I think the matter may have been implicit in instructions on prayer. But it is now made explicit as a philosophy of life—a much more encompassing statement.

> R. Hananiah, Prefect of the Priests, says, "Pray for the welfare of the government. For if it were not for fear of it, one man would swallow his fellow alive."
> R. Hananiah b. Teradion says, "[If] two sit together and between them do not pass teachings of the Torah, lo, this is a seat of the scornful, as it is said, 'Nor sits in the seat of the scornful' (Psalms 1:1). But two who are sitting, and words of the Torah do pass between them—the Presence is with them, as it is said, 'Then they that feared the Lord spoke with one another, and the Lord hearkened and heard, and a book of remembrance was written before him, for them that feared the Lord and gave thought to his name' (Malachi 3:16)." I know that this applies to two. How do I know that even if a single person sits and works on the Torah, the Holy One, blessed be He, set aside a reward for him? As it is said, "Let him sit alone and keep silent, because he has laid it upon him" (Lamentations 3:28).

The reference to God as Presence surely justifies our seeing God here as person, who attends upon the conversations of mortals, hears and responds to what is said. Here too we find Torah study treated as the Mishnah treats prayer. The attitudes required for the one are now demanded for the other. The broadening of the personhood of God takes place in this movement outward from words of prayer to words of Torah study. Study is treated as counterpart to praying, a position not suggested by the authorship of the Mishnah.

> R. Simeon says, "Three who ate at a single table and did not talk about teachings of the Torah while at that table are as though they ate from dead sacrifices (Psalms 106:28), as it is said, 'For all tables are full of vomit and filthiness [if they are] without God' (Isaiah 28:8). But three who ate at a

single table and did talk about teachings of the Torah while at that table are
as if they ate at the table of the Omnipresent, blessed is he, as it is said,
'And he said to me, This is the table that is before the Lord' (Ezekiel
41:22)."

The point is the same as before, equally explicit and fresh.

R. Hananiah b. Hakhinai says, "He who gets up at night, and he who
walks around by himself, and he who turns his desire to emptiness—lo, this
person is liable for his life."

R. Nehunia b. Haqqaneh says, "From whoever accepts upon himself
the yoke of the Torah do they remove the yoke of the state and the yoke
of hard labor. And upon whoever removes from himself the yoke of the
Torah do they lay the yoke of the state and the yoke of hard labor."

R. Halafta of Kefar Hananiah says, "Among ten who sit and work hard
on the Torah the Presence comes to rest, as it is said, 'God stands in the
congregation of God' (Psalms 82:1). And how do we know that the same
is so even of five? For it is said, 'And he has founded his group upon the
earth' (Amos 9:6). And how do we know that this is so even of three?
Since it is said, 'And he judges among the judges.' (Psalms 82:1). And
how do we know that this is so even of two? Because it is said, 'Then they
that feared the Lord spoke with one another, and the Lord hearkened and
heard' (Malachi 3:16). And how do we know that this is so even of one?
Since it is said, 'In every place where I record my name I will come to you
and I will bless you' (Exodus 20:21)."

The shift from prayer to Torah study once more accounts for the
striking allegation that God is present among all those who engage
in Torah study. God is encountered as person in the Torah as much
as in prayer, and this point is repeated time and again. Obviously,
to these allegations God is critical. But God does not require
extensive description; the person remains essentially premise, but
the generative inquiry attends to other matters, particularly Torah
study. Tractate *Avot* works out its sayings mainly on the twin
themes of study through discipleship and application of the Torah,
serving as a handbook for disciples. To that program God is of
course necessary, but, as to making the points the authorship
wishes to register, also insufficient. God is not represented as a sage;
God is not portrayed as the model for the disciple or master; and

God is not set forth as a student of the Torah. These later motifs never enter the imagination of our authorship. To state the matter simply, God, now seen as the model and likeness by which the human emotions and attitudes take their measure, has yet to undergo that stage of metaphorization that renders God incarnate. To state matters as our sages would, we are like God as to our right attitudes, and God therefore responds to our desires and feelings; but we are not like God as to our very being, our shape and form, our activity and concrete life. We are incarnate in ways that God is not—at least, not yet.

R. Eleazar of Bartota says, "Give him what is his, for you and yours are his. For so does it say about David, 'For all things come of you, and of your own have we given you' (1 Chronicles 29:14)."

This saying presents no surprises, affirming, as it does, God's right of possession of all things.

R. Simeon says, "He who is going along the way and repeating [his Torah tradition] but interrupts his repetition and says, 'How beautiful is that tree! How beautiful is that ploughed field!'—Scripture reckons it to him as if he has become liable for his life."

R. Dosetai b. R. Yannai in the name of R. Meir says, "Whoever forgets a single thing from what he has learned—Scripture reckons it to him as if he has become liable for his life, as it is said, 'Only take heed to yourself and keep your soul diligently, lest you forget the words which your eyes saw' (Deuteronomy 4:9)." Is it possible that this is so even if his learning became too much for him? Scripture says, "Lest they depart from your heart all the days of your life." Thus he becomes liable for his life only when he will sit down and actually remove [his learning] from his own heart.

R. Haninah b. Dosa says, "For anyone whose fear of sin takes precedence over his wisdom, his wisdom will endure. And for anyone whose wisdom takes precedence over his fear of sin, his wisdom will not endure."

He would say, "Anyone whose deeds are more than his wisdom—his wisdom will endure. And anyone whose wisdom is more than his deeds—his wisdom will not endure."

He would say, "Anyone from whom people take pleasure—the Omnipresent takes pleasure. And anyone from whom people do not take pleasure, the Omnipresent does not take pleasure."

God's attitudes prove congruent with those of a human being. God then is comparable, once more seen as a person, not merely a premise of being, and our feelings are like God's feelings.

R. Dosa b. Harkinas says, "Sleeping late in the morning, drinking wine at noon, chatting with children, and attending the synagogues of the ignorant drive a man out of the world."

R. Eleazar the Modite says, "He who treats Holy Things as secular, and he who despises the appointed times, he who humiliates his fellow in public, he who removes the signs of the covenant [that is, the mark of circumcision] of Abraham, our father, (may he rest in peace), and he who exposes aspects of the Torah not in accord with the law, even though he has in hand learning in the Torah and good deeds, will have no share in the world to come."

R. Ishmael says, "Be quick [in service] to a superior, efficient in service [to the state], and receive everybody with joy."

R. Akiva says, "Laughter and lightheadedness turn lewdness into a habit. Tradition is a fence for the Torah. Tithes are a fence for wealth. Vows are a fence for abstinence. A fence for wisdom is silence."

He would say, "Precious is the human being, who was created in the image [of God]. It was an act of still greater love that it was made known to him that he was created in the image [of God], as it is said, 'For in the image of God he made man' (Genesis 9:6).

"Precious are Israelites, who are called children to the Omnipresent. It was an act of still greater love that it was made known to them that they were called children to the Omnipresent, as it is said, 'You are the children of the Lord your God' (Deuteronomy 14:1).

"Precious are Israelites, to whom was given the precious thing. It was an act of still greater love that it was made known to them that to them was given that precious thing with which the world was made, as it is said, 'For I give you a good doctrine. Do not forsake my Torah' (Proverbs 4:2)."

God's love—like the love of a human being—takes form in God's informing humanity, in particular Israel, of that love. Once more God is given personhood, with traits remarkably like those of the human being who forms the model or the ideal of our authorship. The step yet to be taken would turn the shared psychological traits into a common incarnate being, God as engaged personality. That would be a while in coming. And when it did come, God would play a far more central role in the exposition of diverse authorships than we find assigned to God in tractate *Avot*. From here to the end of the document, the focus remains where our authorship wants it, which is on study of the Torah, discipleship, relationship of deed and deliberation, issues important to circles of sages. To the discourse that follows, God is necessary but insufficient.

"Everything is foreseen, and free choice is given. In goodness the world is judged. And all is in accord with the abundance of deed[s]."

He would say, "All is handed over as a pledge. And a net is cast over all the living. The store is open, the storekeeper gives credit, the account book is open, and the hand is writing.

"Whoever wants to borrow may come and borrow. The charity collectors go around every day and collect from man whether he knows it or not. And they have grounds for what they do. And the judgment is a true judgment. And everything is ready for the meal."

R. Eleazar b. Azariah says, "If there is no learning of the Torah, there is no proper conduct. If there is no proper conduct, there is no learning in the Torah. If there is no wisdom, there is no reverence. If there is no reverence, there is no wisdom. If there is no understanding, there is no knowledge. If there is no knowledge, there is no understanding. If there is no sustenance, there is no Torah learning. If there is no Torah learning, there is no sustenance."

He would say, "Anyone whose wisdom is greater than his deeds—to what is he to be likened? To a tree with abundant foliage but few roots. When the winds come, they will uproot it and blow it down, as it is said, 'He shall be like a tamarisk in the desert and shall not see when good comes, but shall inhabit the parched places in the wilderness' (Jeremiah 17:6). But anyone whose deeds are greater than his wisdom—to what is he to be likened? To a tree with little foliage but abundant roots. For even if all the winds in the world were to come and blast at it, they will not move it from its place, as it is said, 'He shall be as a tree planted by the waters, and that spreads out its roots by the river, and shall not fear when heat comes, and his leaf shall be green, and shall not be careful in the year of drought, neither shall cease from yielding fruit' (Jeremiah 17:8)."

R. Eleazar Hisma says, "The laws of bird-offerings and of the beginning of the menstrual period—they are indeed the essentials of the Torah. Calculation of the equinoxes and reckoning the numerical value of letters are the savories of wisdom."

Chapter 4

Ben Zoma says, "Who is a sage? He who learns from everybody, as it is said, 'From all my teachers I have gotten understanding' (Psalms 119:99).

Who is strong? He who overcomes his desire, as it is said, 'He who is slow to anger is better than the mighty, and he who rules his spirit than he who takes a city' (Proverbs 16:32). Who is rich? He who is happy in what he has, as it is said, 'When you eat the labor of your hands, happy will you be, and it will go well with you' (Psalms 128:2). (Happy will you be—in this world, and it will go well with you—in the world to come.) Who is honored? He who honors everybody, as it is said, 'For those who honor me I shall honor, and they who despise me will be treated as of no account' (1 Samuel 2:30)."

Ben Azzai says, "Run after the most minor religious duty as after the most important, and flee from transgression. For doing one religious duty draws in its wake doing yet another, and doing one transgression draws in its wake doing yet another. For the reward of doing a religious duty is a religious duty, and the reward of doing a transgression is a transgression."

He would say, "Do not despise anybody and do not treat anything as unlikely. For you have no one who does not have his time, and you have nothing which does not have its place."

R. Levitas of Yavneh says, "Be exceedingly humble, for the future of humanity is the worm."

R. Yohanan b. Beroqa says, "Whoever secretly treats the Name of Heaven as profane publicly pays the price. All the same are the one who does so inadvertently and the one who does so deliberately, when it comes to treating the name of Heaven as profane."

Divine justice is given a concrete form. God responds to the way in which "the name of heaven" is treated.

R. Ishmael, his son, says, "He who learns so as to teach—they give him a chance to learn and to teach. He who learns so as to carry out his teachings—they give him a chance to learn, to teach, to keep, and to do."

R. Sadoq says, "Do not make [Torah teachings] a crown in which to glorify yourself or a spade with which to dig. (So did Hillel say, 'He who uses the crown perishes.') Thus have you learned: Whoever derives worldly benefit from teachings of the Torah takes his life out of this world."

Right attitude toward heaven defines right attitude toward Torah study, and correct intentionality once more forms the centerpiece of the whole.

R. Yose says, "Whoever honors the Torah himself is honored by people. And whoever disgraces the Torah himself is disgraced by people."

R. Ishmael, his son, says, "He who avoids serving as a judge avoids the power of enmity, robbery, and false swearing. And he who is arrogant about making decisions is a fool, evil, and prideful."

He would say, "Do not serve as a judge by yourself, for there is only One who serves as a judge all alone. And do not say, 'Accept my opinion,' for they have the choice in the matter, not you."

R. Jonathan says, "Whoever keeps the Torah when poor will in the end keep it in wealth. And whoever treats the Torah as nothing when he is wealthy in the end will treat it as nothing in poverty."

R. Meir says, "Keep your business to a minimum and make your business the Torah. And be humble before everybody. And if you treat the Torah as nothing, you will have many treating you as nothing. And if you have labored in the Torah, [the Torah] has a great reward to give you."

R. Eleazar b. Jacob says, "He who does even a single religious duty gets himself a good advocate. He who does even a single transgression gets himself a powerful prosecutor. Penitence and good deeds are like a shield against punishment."

R. Yohanan Hasandelar says, "Any gathering which is for the sake of Heaven is going to endure. And any which is not for the sake of Heaven is not going to endure."

R. Eleazar b. Shammua says, "The honor owing to your disciple should be as precious to you as yours. And the honor owing to your fellow should be like the reverence owing to your master. And the reverence owing to your master should be like the awe owing to Heaven."

By this point the implications scarcely require articulation. One's right attitude toward Heaven takes shape in the model of the right attitude of a slave toward the master: awe, obedience, duty. In such a pattern God as person is fully present.

R. Judah says, "Be meticulous about learning, for error in learning leads to deliberate [violation of the Torah]."

R. Simeon says, "There are three crowns: the crown of the Torah, the crown of priesthood, and the crown of sovereignty. But the crown of a good name is best of them all."

R. Nehorai says, "Go into exile to a place of the Torah, and do not suppose that it will come to you. For your fellow disciples will make it solid in your hand. And on your own understanding do not rely."

R. Yannai says, "We do not have in hand [an explanation] either for the prosperity of the wicked or for the suffering of the righteous."

R. Matya b. Harash says, "Greet everybody first, and be a tail to lions. But do not be a head of foxes."

R. Jacob says, "This world is like an antechamber before the world to come. Get ready in the antechamber, so you can go into the great hall."

He would say, "Better is a single moment spent in penitence and good deeds in this world than the whole of the world to come. And better is a single moment of inner peace in the world to come than the whole of a lifetime spent in this world."

R. Simeon b. Eleazar says, "Do not try to make amends with your fellow when he is angry, or comfort him when the corpse of his beloved is lying before him, or seek to find absolution for him at the moment at which he takes a vow, or attempt to see him when he is humiliated."

Samuel the Small says, " 'Rejoice not when your enemy falls, and let not your heart be glad when he is overthrown, lest the Lord see it and it displease him, and he turn away his wrath from him' (Proverbs 24:17)."

Elisha b. Abuyah says, "He who learns when a child—what is he like? Ink put down on a clean piece of paper. And he who learns when an old man—what is he like? Ink put down on a paper full of erasures."

R. Yose b. R. Judah of Kefar Habbabli says, "He who learns from children—what is he like? One who eats sour grapes and drinks fresh wine. And he who learns from old men—what is he like? He who eats ripe grapes and drinks vintage wine."

Rabbi says, "Do not look at the bottle but at what is in it. You can have a new bottle of old wine, and an old bottle which has not even new wine."

R. Eleazar Haqqappar says, "Jealousy, lust, and ambition drive a person out of this world."

He would say, "Those who are born are [destined] to die, and those who die are [destined] for resurrection. And the living are [destined] to be judged—so as to know, to make known, and to confirm that he is God, he is the one who forms, he is the one who creates, he is the one who understands, he is the one who judges, he is the one who gives evidence, he is the one who brings suit, and he is the one who is going to make the ultimate judgment.

"Blessed be he, for before him are no guile, forgetfulness, respect for persons, or bribe taking, for everything is his. And know that everything is subject to reckoning. And do not let your evil impulse persuade you that Sheol is a place of refuge for you. For despite your wishes were you formed, despite your wishes were you born, despite your wishes do you live, despite your wishes do you die, and despite your wishes are you going to give a full accounting before the King of kings of kings, the Holy One blessed be he."

God as person, not merely premise or presence, is richly present here. The God whom we know through the logical, scientific processes of proving that the world exhibits a purposeful order, a hierarchy that leads from all things to the One, and from the One to all things, is far in the background. Now we are told what God is and does, the things one expects from the living and acting God: the ultimate judge. God as the perfect judge, who does not take bribes or respond to cajoling, who demands obedience and duty, emerges as a fully described person. One step remains, and that is the description of God in the concrete terms in which one describes a personality.

PART II

The First Talmud's God in Person

4

God in Person

Had Judaism emerged from the Mishnah, philosophers over the ages would have found themselves with an easy task in setting forth in a systematic and abstract way the doctrine of God and our relationship with God: the first principle, much like the unmoved mover of Greek philosophy, the premise, the presence, and above all the one who made the rules and keeps them in place. And in the context of tractate *Avot,* knowing God through the Torah is something that philosophers find a familiar task. Most people, however, encounter the world not in mind alone but also in heart and soul, not in the processes of thought primarily but mostly in things that happen; they cannot have found the portrait of a presence and a principle entirely pertinent. And that philosophical God would, over time, puzzle the faithful, who found in the written Torah the commandment to "love the Lord your God with all your heart, with all your soul, and with all your might," a commandment not readily carried out in behalf of the unmoved mover, the principle and premise of being. Such a God as the philosophers set forth is to be affirmed and acknowledged, but by knowledge few are changed, and all one's love is not all that easily lavished on an abstract presence. When we come to the Talmud of the Land of Israel we meet God in familiar but also fresh representation.

The writings of sages of the Land of Israel that reached closure at the end of the fourth and beginning of the fifth century, the Talmud of the Land of Israel, a massive commentary to thirty-nine of the sixty-three tractates of the Mishnah, recast and enriched the received Oral Torah. This reconsideration and re-presentation of matters responded to a critical challenge. In the early part of the fourth century, Roman Emperor Constantine made Christianity a licit religion, and by the end of that same century, Christianity, representing itself as the completion and fulfillment of ancient Israel's revelation and prophecies, had become the state religion of the Roman Empire.

The symbolic system of Christianity, with Christ triumphant, with the cross as the regnant symbol, with the canon of Christianity now defined and recognized as authoritative, called forth from the sages of the Land of Israel a symbolic system strikingly responsive to the crisis. Our sages of blessed memory laid renewed stress upon three matters: (1) the coming of the Messiah set as the teleology of the system of Judaism as they defined that system, (2) the symbol of the Torah expanded to encompass the whole of human existence as the system laid forth the limns of that existence, (3) the canon of Sinai broadened to take account of the entirety of the sages' teachings, as much as of the Written Torah that everyone acknowledged as authoritative. In that same context, the representation of God in man, god incarnate in Jesus Christ, as the Christians saw him, found a powerful reply in the re-presentation of God as person, individual and active. God is no longer only, or mainly, the premise of all being, nor is God only or mainly the one who makes the rules and enforces them. God is now presented in the additional form of the one who makes decisions in the here and now of every day life, responding to the individual and his or her actions. Not only so, but the actions of an individual are treated one by one, in the specific context of the person, and not all together in the general context of the social world overall. And, as we saw in the Mishnah, that is not the primary activity of God at all.

Before proceeding in Chapter 5 to the genuinely fresh experience of God, contained within the doctrine of *zekhut,* that is recorded in the sages' writings that came to a conclusion after the Christianization of Rome, let us briefly reconsider the familiar ones, beginning with God as a premise. The fact that God gave the Torah, of course, forms a premise of all discourse, but God's person or personality in giving the Torah is not set forth. So, too, it is taken for granted that God, as ruler of all, assigned traits to this one or to that; for example, "The Holy One, blessed be he, gave to Israel three good qualities: modesty, kindness, and caring" (Yerushalmi *Sanhedrin* 6:7). Along these same lines, God, or Heaven, is responsible for sending rain, as in the following colloquy between a holy man, who can bring rain, and our sages:

Yerushalmi Taanit

He came down to them and asked, "Why have the rabbis troubled themselves to come here today?"
They said to him, "We want you to pray for rain."
He said to them, "Now do you really need my prayers? Heaven has already done its miracle."

Obviously, the premise is that God has done the miracle of making rain without the wonder-worker's intervention. But the passage does not invoke the presence or person of God in particular; it makes exactly the opposite point, that there is nothing distinctive about the event. Countless passages of such a character restate the simple fact that God forms the premise of all discourse in the Yerushalmi, as in the other writings of the canon of the Judaism of the Dual Torah.

Overall, however, that fact does not yield a rich statement of God as premise. For instance, God's act of revealing the Torah is not augmented or amplified. Rather, we find the passive, such as: "All those forty days that Moses served on the mountain, he studied the Torah but forgot it. In the end it was given to him as a gift" (Yerushalmi *Horayot* 3:4). God, of course, not only gave the Torah but also enforced its laws. That premise of all discourse hardly has to be proven. Just punishment for sin, just reward for merit—these are ordinary facts of life under God's rule. God rules over land and sea, but we have no stories about God's doing so in person (cf., e.g., Yerushalmi *Abodah Zarah* 4:1): "An earthly king rules only on dry land but not on the sea, but the Holy One . . . is not so. He is ruler by sea and ruler by land."

In the following passage, God serves as the origin of all great teachings, but as we have seen, that fact bears no consequences for the description of God as a person or personality:

Yerushalmi Sanhedrin

"Given by one shepherd"—
Said the Holy One, blessed be he, "If you hear a teaching from an

Israelite minor, and it gave pleasure to you, let it not be in your sight as if
one has heard it from a minor, but as if one has heard it from an adult,

"and let it not be as if one has heard it from an adult, but as if one has
heard it from a sage,

"and let it not be as if one has heard it from a sage, but as if one has
heard it from a prophet,

"and let it not be as if one has heard it from a prophet, but as if one has
heard it from the shepherd,

"and there is as a shepherd only Moses, in line with the following
passage: 'Then he remembered the days of old, of Moses his servant.
Where is he who brought out of the sea the shepherds of his flock? Where
is he who put in the midst of them his holy Spirit?' (Isaiah 63:11).

"It is not as if one has heard it from the shepherd but as if one has heard
it from the Almighty."

"Given by one Shepherd"—and there is only One who is the Holy One,
blessed be he, in line with that which you read in Scripture: "Hear, O
Israel: the Lord our God is one Lord" (Deuteronomy 6:4).

In studying the Torah, sages and disciples clearly met the living God
and recorded a direct encounter with and experience of God
through God's revealed word. But in a statement such as this,
alluding to but not clearly describing what it means to hear the
word of the Almighty, God at the end of the line simply forms the
premise of revelation. There is no further effort at characterization.
The exposition of the work of Creation (Yerushalmi *Hagigah* 2:1)
refers to God's deeds, mainly by citing verses of Scripture: "Then
he made the snow: 'He casts forth his ice like morsels' (Psalms
147:17)," and so on. So too God has wants and desires—for
example, what God wants is for Israel to repent, at which time God
will save Israel (Yerushalmi *Taanit* 1:1)—but there is no effort to
characterize God.

God is understood as establishing a presence in the world. This is
accomplished through intermediaries such as a retinue of angels and
also through the hypostatization of divine attributes, such as the
Holy Spirit, the Presence of *Shekhinah,* and the like. The Holy
Spirit makes its appearance, as in "They were delighted that their
opinion proved to be the same as that of the Holy Spirit"
(Yerushalmi *Horayot* 3:5, *Abodah Zarah* 3:1 and so on). God is
understood to enjoy a retinue, a court (*Sanhedrin* 1:1); God's seal is
truth. These and similar statements restate the notion that God

forms a living presence in the world. Heaven reaches decisions and conveys them to humankind through the working of chance, as in a lottery:

Yerushalmi Sanhedrin 1:4

To whomever turned up in his hand a slip marked, "Elder," he said, "they have indeed chosen you in Heaven." To whomever turned up in his hand a blank slip, he would say, "What can I do for you? It is from Heaven."

The notion that the lottery conveys God's will, and therefore represents God's presence in the decision-making process, would not have surprised the authorship of the book of Esther. It is one way in which God's presence is given concrete form. Another way, also supplied by Scripture, posited that God in the very Presence intervened in Israel's history, such as at the Sea of Reeds:

Sanhedrin 2:1

When the All-Merciful came forth to redeem Israel from Egypt, he did not send a messenger or an angel, but the Holy One, blessed be he, himself came forth, as it is said, "For I will pass through the Land of Egypt that night" (Exodus 12:12)—and not only so, but it was he and his entire retinue.

The familiar idea that God's presence went into Exile with Israel recurs (*Taanit* 1:1), but I do not know of a single passage in the entire Yerushalmi in which it is claimed that God's personal presence at a historical event in the time of sages changed the course of events. The notion that God's presence remained in Exile leaves God without personality or even ample description.

Where God does take up a presence, it is not uncommonly a literary device, with no important narrative implications. For example, God is assumed to speak through any given verse of Scripture. Therefore the first person will be introduced in connection with citing such a verse, as at *Sanhedrin* 5:1: "[God answers,] 'It was an act of love which I did . . . [citing a verse,] for I said, "The world will be built upon merciful love" ' (Psalms 89:3)."

Here since the cited verse has an "I," God is given a presence in the colloquy. But it is a mere formality. So too we may say that God has made such and such a statement, which serves not to characterize God but only to supply an attribution for an opinion:

Nedarim 6:9

It is written, "These are the words of the letter which Jeremiah . . . sent from Jerusalem to the rest of the elders of the exiles" (Jeremiah 29:1).
Said the Holy One, blessed be he, "The elders of the exile are valuable to me. Yet more beloved to me is the smallest circle which is located in the Land of Israel than a great sanhedrin located outside of the Land."

All we have here is a paraphrase and restatement of the cited verse.

Where actions are attributed to God, we of course have to recognize God's presence in context, as in "The Holy One, blessed be he, kept to himself [and did not announce] the reward that is coming to those who carry out their religious duties, so that they should do them in true faith [without expecting a reward]" (*Qiddushin* 1:7). But such a statement hardly constitutes evidence that God is present and active in a given circumstance. It rather forms into a personal statement the principle that one should do religious duties for the right motive, not expecting a reward—a view we found commonplace in Mishnah tractate *Avot*. So too statements of God's action carry slight characterization, such as, "Even if 999 aspects of the argument of an angel incline against someone, but a single aspect of the case of that angel argues in favor, the Holy One . . . still inclines the scales in favor of the accused" (Yerushalmi *Qiddushin* 1:9). It remains to observe that when we find in the Yerushalmi a sizable narrative of intensely important events, such as the destruction of Betar in the time of Bar Kokhba (*Taanit* 4:5), God scarcely appears except, again, as premise and source of all that happens. There is no characterization, nor even the claim that God intervened in some direct and immediate way, though I do not believe we can imagine that anyone thought otherwise. That simple affirmation reaches expression, for instance, in the following observation, in connection with the destruction of the Temple: "It appears that the Holy One, blessed be he, wants to exact from our hand vengeance for his blood" (*Taanit* 4:5). That sort of intrusion hardly suggests a vivid presence of God as part of the narrative scheme, let alone a characterization of God as person.

Sages in the Yerushalmi may have made up conversations between biblical heroes and God, but when it came to their own day, such conversations took the form of prayers. As to the former:

Peah 1:1 (translation by Roger Brooks)

At that very moment, David said to the Holy One, blessed be he, "Master of the Universe, shall your presence descend upon the earth? May your presence rise up from among them! . . ." [David is urging God to remain over the earth and not among gossip-mongers on earth.]

In this case, a conversation between God and David is made up; I cannot point in the Yerushalmi to equivalent conversations involving sages.

But of course God does occur as a "you" throughout the Yerushalmi, most commonly in a liturgical setting. As in the earlier documents of the oral part of the Torah, so in the Yerushalmi, we have a broad range of prayers to God as "you," illustrated by the following:

Berakhot 1:4 (translation by Tzvee Zahavy)

R. Ba bar Zabeda in the name of Rab: "[The congregation says this prayer in an undertone:] 'We give thanks to you, for we must praise your name. My lips will shout for joy when I sing praises to you, my soul also which you have rescued' (Psalms 71:23). Blessed are you, Lord, God of praises.' "

Since the formula of the blessing invokes "you," we find nothing surprising in the liturgical person imagined by the framers of various prayers. God's ad hoc intervention, as an active and participating personality, in specific situations is treated as more or less a formality, in that the rules are given and will come into play without ordinarily requiring God to join in a given transaction:

Berakhot 4:2 (translation by Tzvee Zahavy)

When one enters the study hall, what does he say? "May it be your will, Lord my God, God of my fathers, that I shall not be angry with my colleagues and they not be angry with me; that we not declare what is clean to be unclean and vice versa; that we not declare what is permitted to be forbidden and vice versa; lest I find myself put to shame in this world and in the world to come."

Here we see yet another fine instance in which God is a "you" but in which that "you" does not intervene in a particular case or engage in a concrete, ad hoc transaction. "May it be your will . . . ," a standard liturgical formula, never is followed by a tale showing how, on a specific occasion, God showed that that was, indeed, the divine will (or the opposite). God was encountered as a very real presence, actively listening to prayers, as in the following:

Berakhot 9:1

See how high the Holy One, blessed be he, is above his world. Yet a person can enter a synagogue, stand behind a pillar, and pray in an undertone, and the Holy One, blessed be he, hears his prayers, as it says, "Hannah was speaking in her heart; only her lips moved, and her voice was not heard" (1 Samuel 1:13). Yet the Holy One, blessed be he, heard her prayer.

When, however, we distinguish God as person, "you," from God as a well-portrayed active personality, liturgical formulas give a fine instance of the one side of the distinction. In the Yerushalmi's sizable corpus of such prayers, both individual and community, we never find testimony to a material change in God's decision in a case in which God sets aside known rules in favor of an episodic act of intervention, and it follows that thought on God as person remains continuous with what has gone before. Sages, like everyone else in Israel, believed that God hears and answers prayer, but that belief did not require them to preserve stories about specific instances in which this hearing and answering attested to a particular personality trait or character being imputed to God. A specific episode or incident never served to highlight the characterization of divinity in one particular way, in a manner parallel to Scripture's authorships' use of stories to portray God as a sharply etched personality.

For yet another example of God as person in a liturgical passage, Yerushalmi *Taanit* 2:1 (among many instances) uses the imperative: "[They sound the horns] as if to say, 'Consider us as if we cry like a beast before you.' " But in the personification of God, referred to in context as "Lord of the world," we find very few sustained conversations in which God takes an active role in discourse. An example of the essentially passive character of God as "you" is in the following:

Sanhedrin 2:6

R. Simeon b. Yohai taught, "The book of Deuteronomy went up and spread itself out before the Holy One, blessed be he, saying before him, 'Lord of the world! You have written in your Torah that any covenant, part of which is null is wholly nullified. Now lo, Solomon wishes to uproot a Y of mine.' Said to him the Holy One, blessed be he, 'Solomon and a thousand like him will be null, but not one word of yours will be nullified.' "

Here, as commonly is the case, the depiction of God follows the logic of the story. God has no particular traits imputed by the narrative, rather serving as a conversation partner for the book of Deuteronomy. Still, God is portrayed as a person, not merely a presence.

One aspect of personhood is capacity to carry out deeds, and it goes without saying that in the document at hand God is represented as doing things, past, present, and future. For example:

Shabbat 6:9

R. Berekhiah in the name of R. Abba bar Kahan: "In the future, the Holy One, blessed be he, is going to set the place of the righteous closer to his throne than the place of the ministering angels. The ministering angels will ask them and say to them, 'What has God wrought?' (Numbers 23:23). That is, what did the Holy One, blessed be he, teach you?"

Said R. Levi bar Hayyuta, "Did he not do so in this world? . . ."

God's doing this or that forms part of a larger portrait of God as a person capable of carrying out purposive deeds. When, presently, we meet God as a fully etched personality, God will be shown to do the deeds human beings do in the way that human beings do them. At this point, by contrast, even a very long catalogue of the great deeds of God cannot yield much of a picture of God as a "you," a person people may know and love.

Not only so, but the representation in the Yerushalmi of God as a person does not fully work out the potential of a given subject that invites it. For example, God is angry, so Scripture says, on account of idolatry. Yet in the Yerushalmi's exposition of the pertinent chapters of *Abodah Zarah*, beginning with Chapter 3, for example, I find not a single story of God's anger embodied in a picture of God as a person, let alone as a personality. The matter is left as a prevailing attitude or principle. When God does appear, it is as an essentially passive participant, such as the conversation partner who asks, "Why?" or who confirms what the protagonist proposes, as in the following:

Sanhedrin 10:2

But the Holy One, blessed be he, said to Elijah, "This Hiel is a great man. Go and see him [because his sons have died]."
He said to him, "I am not going to see him."
He said to him, "Why?"
He said to him, "For if I go and they say things which will outrage you, I shall not be able to bear it."
He said to him, "Then if they say things which outrage me, whatever you decree against them I shall carry out."

Here God is person and not abstract principle or premise, but still not a vividly etched personality. The conversation is an exchange of conventional theological positions, not a transaction between two distinctive personalities, each entering into a one-time exchange with the other. Another example of the same phenomenon from *Sanhedrin*:

It is written, "Then the word of the Lord came to Isaiah: 'Go and say to Hezekiah, Thus says the Lord, the God of David your father: I have heard your prayer, I have seen your tears; behold I will add fifteen years to your life' " (Isaiah 38:4–5).

[Isaiah] said to him, "Thus I've already told him, and how thus do I say to him? He is a man occupied with great affairs, and he will not believe me."

[God] said to him, "He is a very humble man, and he will believe you. And not only so, but as yet the rumor has not yet gone forth in the city."

"And before Isaiah had gone out of the middle court, [the word of the Lord came to him]" (2 Kings 20:4).

Here once again God is a mere conversation partner, a straight man once more, pointing to facts already established in context and not doing more than moving the narrative along by word or deed. When God serves as the protagonist of a story and leads the conversation, and when God's part in the conversation is particular to that context and not simply the proclamation of well-known theological principles, then we shall meet God as a fully spelled out and individual personality: divinity in the form of humanity. But it is not so in the present compilation, so far as I have been able to discover. Yet another case is in the same context:

Sanhedrin 10:2

Now all the ministering angels went and closed the windows, so that the prayer of Manasseh should not reach upward to the Holy One, blessed be he.

The ministering angels were saying before the Holy One, blessed be he, "Lord of the world, a man who worshipped idols and put up an image in the Temple—are you going to accept him back as a penitent?"

He said to them, "If I do not accept him back as a penitent, lo, I shall lock the door before all penitents."

What did the Holy One, blessed be he, do? He made an opening [through the heavens] under his throne of glory and listened to his supplication.

That is in line with the following verse of Scripture: "He prayed to him, and God received his entreaty and heard his supplication and brought him again [to Jerusalem into his kingdom]. [Then Manasseh knew that the Lord was God]" (2 Chronicles 33:13).

Here we have a more concrete characterization of a deed done by God, which shows God's character as merciful. Yet another passage that shows the same tendency is as follows:

Makkot

Said R. Phineas, " 'Good and upright is the Lord. Therefore he instructs sinners in the way' (Psalms 25:8). Why is he good? Because he is upright. And why upright? Because he is good. 'Therefore he instructs sinners in the way' by teaching them the way to repentance."
They asked Wisdom, "As to a sinner, what is his punishment?"
She said to them, "Evil pursues the evil" (Proverbs 13:21).
They asked Prophecy, "As to a sinner, what is his punishment?"
She said to them, "The soul that sins shall die" (Ezekiel 18:20).
They asked the Holy One, blessed be he, "As to a sinner, what is his punishment?"
He said to them, "Let the sinner repent, and his sin will be forgiven for him, as it is said, 'Therefore he instructs sinners in the way' (Psalms 25:8). He shows sinners the way to repentance."

This is a further excellent example of how God as person represents a mere hypostatization, without concrete and particular traits. When God is represented as a "you," it turns out (thus far) to form a mere formality of rhetoric.

Imputing thoughts or public statements to God therefore does not much change the picture, as in the following:

Taanit 2:1

Said R. Levi, "What is the meaning of slow to 'anger'?
"The matter may be compared to a king who had two tough legions. He said, 'If they live here with me in the capital, if the city-folk anger me, they will immediately put them down with brute force. I shall send them a long way away, so that if the city folk anger me, while I am yet summoning the legions, the people will appease me and I shall accept their plea.'
"Likewise, the Holy One, blessed be he, said, 'Anger and wrath are angels of destruction. Lo, I shall send them a long way away, and if Israel

angers me, while I am summoning and bringing them to me, Israel will repent and I shall accept their repentance.' "

God may further serve as an active voice, but only in the paraphrase of an available verse of Scripture, as in the following:

Berakhot 5:2

Said R. Judah b. Pazzi, "[God said,] 'That [dew] which I gave as a bequest which may be nullified to Abraham, I give [to his descendants as a gift which can never be nullified],' "May God give you of the dew of heaven" (Genesis 27:28).

Here we have assigned to God simply an amplification of the cited verse of Scripture. Yet another case in which God speaks without emerging as a well-etched personality is the following:

Shekalim 2:6

Said R. Samuel bar Nahman, "Said the Holy One, blessed be he, to David, 'David, I shall count out for you a full complement of days. I shall not give you less than the full number. Will Solomon, your son, not build the Temple in order to offer sacrifices in it? But more proud to me are the just and righteous deeds which you do than the offerings which will be made in the Temple.' "

Numerous examples will not vastly change the picture. God is represented as a person, but not as much of a personality. God's rulings, rather than God's attitudes or emotions or deeds in a concrete narrative, are simply restated in dialogue form, so they do not provide a rich characterization at all.

A statement made by God in the first person is nothing more than a restatement of the point of the parable and does not, therefore, constitute a characterization of God in a specific framework. The reason I think so is that if the storyteller had spoken in the third person, using simply "the Holy One," in no way would the course of the story have shifted. The point of the story lies in imputing to the divinity the trait of patience, not in describing a patient personality in some particular context. Furthermore, even when parables are drawn, they commonly illustrate principles or traits rather than characterize a highly individual personality. For example, in the following parable God is shown to be more loyal as a patron than is a human counterpart. But this turns out merely to illustrate a point Scripture has made and hardly serves to etch in words a vivid personality.

Berakhot 9:1 (translation by Tzvee Zahavy)

R. Yudan in the name of R. Isaac gave four discourses: "A person had a human patron. One day they came and told the patron, 'A member of your household has been arrested.'
"He said to them, 'Let me take his place.'
"They said to him, 'Lo, he is already going out to trial.'
"He said to them, 'Let me take his place.'
"They said to him, 'Lo, he is going to be hanged.'
"Now where is he, and where his patron?
"But the Holy One, blessed be he, [will save his subjects just as he] saved Moses from the sword of Pharaoh. This is in accord with what is written, 'He delivered me from the sword of Pharaoh' (Exodus 18:4)."

The passage goes through a sequence of examples deriving from Scripture of the same fact, namely, God's personal salvation of the saints. God is further portrayed as loyal and humble, identifying with Israel even in their poverty, ignorance, and humiliation. But at no point in the exposition do we find either an immediate case, deriving from sages' own time, or, more to the point, a clear characterization of God in specific and vivid terms. God acts, as Scripture has made clear, and evidence of God's will and person all derive from Scripture. For instance, while everyone believed God answers prayers, where evidence of that fact is adduced, it is from Scripture's cases:

Berakhot 9:3 (translation by Tzvee Zahavy)

Said R. Judah b. Pazzi, "Even if a woman in labor is already seated in the delivery chair, God can change the sex of the foetus, in accord with the verse, 'Behold like clay in the hand of the potter, so you are in my hand, O house of Israel' (Jeremiah 18:6).''

Rabbi in the name of the house of Yannai: "Originally Dinah was a male. After Rachel prayed, she was changed into a female. So it says, 'Afterwards she bore a daughter and called her Dinah' (Genesis 30:21). It was after Rachel prayed that Dinah was changed into a female.''

The evidence is then expounded wholly within the framework of principles established by biblical facts, without a further effort to transform these facts into the portrait of a living personality. God emerges as a person, vital and alive in the life of Israel, but in no way incarnate in everyday encounters, in stories of a personality people might know and engage in conversation.

Now that we have surveyed familiar territory, let us stand back and examine matters from a different perspective altogether. When we asked about the Mishnah's presentation of God, we began with not specific statements but a general question concerning the character of the document as a whole: what do the authors of the Mishnah propose to say over and over again? The answer to that question—that many things resolve into one thing, and that from one thing emanate many things—showed us what the Mishnah says about God everywhere and throughout, mostly when it is not speaking about God at all. So can we now ask the same question: What is principal in the Judaic world of the Talmud of the Land of Israel, and can that fundamental and pervasive conception guide us to a deeper insight into the Yerushalmi's representation of God?

The answer to that question is contained in a single word, *zekhut*, which refers to our capacity for uncoerced action, and the result of God's response to that uncoerced action. That category, which on the face of it refers to moral conduct, in fact formed the foundation for the Yerushalmi's conception of political economy for the social order of Israel. It defined economics and politics—an economics and a politics that made powerlessness into power, disinheritance into wealth. The structure of Israel's political economy therefore rested upon divine response to acts of will consisting of voluntary submission to the will of Heaven; these acts, as we shall see, endowed Israel with a lien and entitlement upon Heaven. What we cannot by will impose, we can by will evoke. What we cannot accomplish through coercion, we can achieve through submission.

God will do for us what we cannot do for ourselves, when we do for God what God cannot make us do. In a wholly concrete and tangible sense, love God with all the heart, the soul, and the might that we have. God then stands above the rules of the created world, because God will respond not only to what we do in conformity to the rules, but also to what we do beyond the requirement of the rules. God is above the rules, and we can gain a response from God when, on some unique occasion, we too do more than obey—when we love, spontaneously and all at once, with the whole of our being. That is the conception of God that *zekhut,* as a conception of power in Heaven and power in humanity, contains. In the relationship between God and humanity expressed in the conception of *zekhut,* we finally reach the understanding of what the Torah means when it tells us that we are in God's image and after God's likeness: we are then, "in our image," the very mirror-image of God. What can that possibly mean? And what can that tell us about God?

5

*From Rule to Exception:
God Makes Choices*

Zekhut stands for the empowerment, of a supernatural character, that derives from the virtue of one's ancestry or from one's own virtuous deeds of a very particular order. No single word in English bears the same meaning, nor can I identify a synonym for *zekhut* in the original canonical writings. The difficulty of translating a word of systemic consequence with a single word in some other language (or in the language of the system's documents themselves) tells us we deal with something unique, beyond comparison and therefore beyond contrast and comprehension. A mark that we have found our way to the systemic center is that we cannot easily translate with a single English equivalent the word that identifies what we conceive to define the system's critical tension and generative concept. What is most particular to the systemic structure and its functioning requires definition through circumlocution, such as I gave earlier: "the heritage of virtue and its consequent entitlements."[1]

Accordingly, the systemic centrality of *zekhut* in the structure, the critical importance of the heritage of virtue together with its

---

[1] The commonly used single word *merit* does not apply, but *merit* bears the sense of reward for carrying out an obligation, as by doing such and such, he merited so and so. *Zekhut*, by contrast, commonly refers to acts of supererogatory free will, and therefore, while such acts are meritorious in the sense of being virtuous (by definition), they are not acts that one owes but rather that one gives. The rewards that accumulate in response to such actions are always miraculous or supernatural or signs of divine grace, such as an unusually long life, or the power to prevent a dilapidated building from collapsing. In a moment I will take up the amplification of the meaning of *zekhut* in response to concrete usages of the word in the earliest document in which it plays a significant role, tractate *Avot,* where it appears in a sufficiently broad context to allow for philological exegesis.

supernatural entitlements—these emerge in a striking claim. It is framed in extreme form—another mark of the unique place of *zekhut* within the system. Here we find a conception that would have posed considerable difficulty to the philosophers: that exceptions to the norm govern, so in the end there is no norm. How is this idea expressed through the concept of *zekhut,* and why do I maintain that, in that expression, we encounter the God whom we may love with all our heart and soul and might—all at once, in a single moment, in the here and now? It is in the conception that even though a man was degraded, one action sufficed to win for him that heavenly glory to which rabbis living lives of Torah study aspired. The mark of the system's integration around *zekhut* lies in its insistence that all Israelites, not only sages, could gain *zekhut* for themselves (and their descendants). A single remarkable deed, exemplary for its deep humanity, sufficed to win for an ordinary person the *zekhut* that elicits supernatural favor. The centrality of *zekhut* in the systemic structure, the critical importance of the heritage of virtue together with its supernatural entitlements emerge in this striking claim. The rabbinical storyteller to whom we shall listen identifies with this lesson.

In all three stories that follow, defining what the individual must do to gain *zekhut,* the point is that the deeds of the heroes make them worthy of having their prayers answered, which is a mark of the working of *zekhut.* It is deeds beyond the strict requirements of the Torah, and even the limits of the law altogether, that transform the hero into a holy man. The following stories should not be understood as expressions of the mere sentimentality of the clerks concerning the lower orders, for in favor of a single action of surpassing power, they deny the sages' lifelong devotion to what was held to be the highest value, knowledge of the Torah:

Yerushalmi Taanit 1:4

A certain man came before one of the relatives of R. Yannai. He said to him, "Rabbi, attain *zekhut* through me [by giving me charity]."

He said to him, "And didn't your father leave you money?"

He said to him, "No."

He said to him, "Go and collect what your father left in deposit with others."

He said to him, "I have heard concerning property my father deposited with others that it was gained by violence [so I don't want it]."

He said to him, "You are worthy of praying and having your prayers answered."

The point, of course, is a reference to the possession of entitlement to supernatural favor, and it is gained, we see, through deeds that the law of the Torah cannot require but must favor: what one does on one's own volition, beyond the measure of the law. Here I see the opposite of sin. A sin is what one has done by one's own volition beyond all limits of the law. So an act that generates *zekhut* for the individual is the counterpart and opposite: what one does by one's own volition that also is beyond all requirements of the law.

A certain ass driver appeared before the rabbis [the context requires: in a dream] and prayed, and rain came. The rabbis sent and brought him and said to him, "What is your trade?"

He said to them, "I am an ass driver."

They said to him, "And how do you conduct your business?"

He said to them, "One time I rented my ass to a certain woman, and she was weeping on the way, and I said to her, 'What's with you?' and she said to me, 'The husband of that woman [me] is in prison [for debt], and I wanted to see what I can do to free him.' So I sold my ass and I gave her the proceeds, and I said to her, 'Here is your money, free your husband, but do not sin [by becoming a prostitute to raise the necessary funds].' "

They said to him, "You are worthy of praying and having your prayers answered."

The ass driver clearly has a powerful lien on Heaven, so his prayers are answered even while those of others are not. What he did to get that entitlement? He did what no law could demand: impoverished himself to save the woman from a "fate worse than death."

In a dream of R. Abbahu, Mr. Pentakaka ["Five sins"] appeared, who prayed that rain would come, and it rained. R. Abbahu sent and summoned him. He said to him, "What is your trade?"

He said to him, "Five sins does that man [I] do every day, [for I am a pimp:] hiring whores, cleaning up the theater, bringing home their garments for washing, dancing, and performing before them."

He said to him, "And what sort of decent thing have you ever done?"

He said to him, "One day that man [I] was cleaning the theater, and a woman came and stood behind a pillar and cried. I said to her, 'What's with you?' And she said to me, 'That woman's [my] husband is in prison, and I wanted to see what I can do to free him,' so I sold my bed and cover, and I gave the proceeds to her. I said to her, 'Here is your money, free your husband, but do not sin.' "

He said to him, "You are worthy of praying and having your prayers answered."

This now moves us still further, since the named man has done everything sinful that one can do, and, more to the point, he does it every day. Thus the singularity of the act of *zekhut,* which suffices if done only one time, encompasses its power to outweigh a life of sin—again, an act of *zekhut* as the mirror image and opposite of sin.

A pious man from Kefar Imi appeared [in a dream] to the rabbis. He prayed for rain and it rained. The rabbis went up to him. His householders told them that he was sitting on a hill. They went out to him, saying to him, "Greetings," but he did not answer them.

He was sitting and eating, and he did not say to them, "You break bread too."

When he went back home, he made a bundle of faggots and put his cloak on top of the bundle [instead of on his shoulder].

When he came home, he said to his household [wife], "These rabbis are here [because] they want me to pray for rain. If I pray and it rains, it is a disgrace for them, and if not, it is a profanation of the Name of Heaven. But come, you and I will go up [to the roof] and pray. If it rains, we shall tell them, 'We are not worthy to pray and have our prayers answered.' "

They went up and prayed and it rained.

They came down to them [and asked], "Why have the rabbis troubled themselves to come here today?"

They said to him, "We wanted you to pray so that it would rain."

He said to them, "Now do you really need my prayers? Heaven already has done its miracle."

They said to him, "Why, when you were on the hill, did we say hello to you, and you did not reply?"

He said to them, "I was then doing my job. Should I then interrupt my concentration [on my work]?"

They said to him, "And why, when you sat down to eat, did you not say to us 'You break bread too'?"

He said to them, "Because I had only my small ration of bread. Why would I have invited you to eat by way of mere flattery [when I knew I could not give you anything at all]?"

They said to him, "And why when you came to go down, did you put your cloak on top of the bundle?"

He said to them, "Because the cloak was not mine. It was borrowed for use at prayer. I did not want to tear it."

They said to him, "And why, when you were on the hill, did your wife wear dirty clothes, but when you came down from the mountain, did she put on clean clothes?"

He said to them, "When I was on the hill, she put on dirty clothes, so that no one would gaze at her. But when I came home from the hill, she put on clean clothes, so that I would not gaze on any other woman."

They said to him, "It is well that you pray and have your prayers answered."

The pious man, finally, enjoys the recognition of the sages by reason of his lien upon Heaven, able as he is to pray and bring rain. What has so endowed him with *zekhut?* Acts of punctiliousness of a moral order: concentrating on his work, avoiding an act of dissimulation, integrity in the disposition of a borrowed object, his wife's concern not to attract other men and her equal concern to make herself attractive to her husband. None of these stories refers explicitly to *zekhut;* all of them tell us about what it means to enjoy not an entitlement by inheritance but a lien accomplished by one's own supererogatory acts of restraint.

The word *zekhut* bears a variety of meanings, as Jastrow summarizes the data,[2] and the pertinence of each possible meaning is to be determined in context: (1) acquittal, plea in favor of the defendant; (2) doing good, blessing; (3) protecting influence of good conduct, merit; (4) advantage, privilege, benefit. The first meaning pertains solely in juridical (or metaphorically juridical) contexts; the second represents a very general and imprecise use of the word, since a variety of other words bear the same meaning. Only the third and the fourth meanings pertain, since they are particular to this word

---

[2]Marcus Jastrow, *A Dictionary of the Targumim, The Talmud Babli* and *Ye-rushalmi, and the Midrashic Literature* (New York: Pardes Publishing House, Inc., reprinted 1950), p. 398.

and also are religious. That is, only through using the word *zekhut* do authors of compositions and authorships of composites express the sense given at definition 3. Moreover, it will rapidly become clear, in context, that definition 4 is not to be distinguished from definition 3, since "protecting influence of good conduct" when the word *zekhut* appears always yields "advantage, privilege, benefit." It follows, for the purposes of systemic analysis, that where the word *zekhut* bears the sense of "the protecting influence of good conduct" which yields "advantage, privilege, or benefit," such passages will tell us how the word *zekhut* functions.

My simple definition (at the beginning of this chapter) emphasizes *heritage,* because the advantages or privileges conferred by *zekhut* may be inherited and also passed on; it stresses *entitlements* because advantages or privileges always result from receiving *zekhut* from ancestors or acquiring it on one's own; and I use the word *virtue* to refer to those supererogatory acts that demand a reward because they form matters of choice, the gift of the individual and his or her act of free will, an act that is at the same time (1) uncompelled, by, for example, the obligations imposed by the Torah, but (2) also valued by the Torah. The systemic importance of the conception of *zekhut* derives from its capacity to unite the generations in a heritage of entitlements; *zekhut* is fundamentally a historical category and concept, in that, like all historical systems of thought, it explains the present in terms of the past, and the future in terms of the present.

Because *zekhut* is something one may receive as an inheritance, out of the distant past, it imposes upon the definition of the social entity, "Israel," a genealogical meaning. It furthermore imparts a distinctive character to the definitions of way of life. Thus the task of the political component of a theory of the social order, which is to define the social entity by appeal to empowerment, and the task of the economic component, which is to identify scarce resources by specification of the rationality of right management, is accomplished in a single word, which stands for a conception, a symbol, and a myth. All three components of this religious theory of the social order turn out to present specific applications, in context, for the general conception of *zekhut*. The first source of *zekhut* derives from the definition of Israel as family; the entitlements of supernatural power deriving from virtue, then, are inherited from Abraham, Isaac, and Jacob. The second source is personal: the power one can gain for one's own heirs, moreover, by virtuous deeds. *Zekhut* deriving from either source is to be defined in context: what can you do if you have *zekhut* that you cannot do if you do not have *zekhut,* and to whom can you do it? The answer to that question tells you the empowerment of *zekhut.*

Now in the nature of things, a theory of power or violence that is legitimately exercised falls into the category of a politics, and a conception of the scarce resource, defined as supernatural power that is to be rationally managed, falls into the category of an economics. That is why in the concept of *zekhut,* we find the union of economics and politics into a political economy: a theory of the whole society in its material and social relationships as expressed in institutions that are given the permanent right to impose order through real or threatened violence and in the assignment of goods and benefits—as systemically defined, to be sure—through a shared rationality.

How shall we then know what belongs and what does not belong if *zekhut* bears the confusing translation of "merit" and if "merit" promiscuously refers to pretty much anything that one gets *not* as one's just desserts at all, but despite what one has done? Scripture, for example, knows that God loves Israel because he loved the patriarchs (Deuteronomy 4:37); the memory or deeds of the righteous patriarchs and matriarchs appear in a broad range of contexts—for example, "Remember your servants, Abraham, Isaac, and Jacob" (Exodus 32:13) for Moses, and "Remember the good deeds of David, your servant" (2 Chronicles 6:42) for David. At stake throughout is giving people what they do not merit, to be sure. But in these contexts, "remembering" what X did as an argument in behalf of favor for Y does not invoke the word *zekhut,* and the context does not require use of that word either. Accordingly, our definition requires limitation to precise usages of a given word. Were we to propose to work our way back from situations that seem to exhibit conceptual affinities to the concept represented by the word under consideration—cases, for instance, in which someone appeals to what is owing the fathers in behalf of the children—we would not accomplish the goal, which is to define a word that, in this system and these documents, bears a particular meaning and, more to the point, carries out a highly critical role.

At Mishnah *Sanhedrin* 4:1, 5:4, 5:5, and 6:1 we find *zekhut* in the sense of "acquittal," as against conviction; at Mishnah *Ketubot* 13:6 the sense is, "right," as in "right of ownership"; at Mishnah *Gittin* 8:8 the sense is not "right of ownership" in a narrow sense, but "advantage," in a broader one of prerogative: "It is not within the power of the first husband to render void the right of the second." These usages, of course, bear no point in common with the sense of the word later on, but the evidence of the Mishnah seems to me to demonstrate that the sense of *zekhut* paramount in the successor documents is not original to them. The following usage at Mishnah *Qiddushin* 4:14 seems to me to invite something very like the sense that I have proposed here:

> R. Meir says, "A man should always teach his son a clean and easy trade. And let him pray to him to whom belong riches and possessions. For there is no trade which does not involve poverty or wealth. For poverty does not come from one's trade, nor does wealth come from one's trade. But all is in accord with a man's *zekhut*."

Exactly how to translate our key word in this passage is not self-evident. The context permits a variety of possibilities. The same usage seems to be located at Mishnah *Sotah* 3:4–5, and here there is clear indication of the conception of an entitlement deriving from some source other than one's own deed of the moment:

Mishnah Sotah 3:4–5

> There is the possibility that *zekhut* suspends the curse for one year, and there is the possibility that *zekhut* suspends the curse for two years, and there is the possibility that *zekhut* suspends the curse for three years.
>
> On this basis Ben Azzai says, "A man is required to teach Torah to his daughter.
>
> "For if she should drink the water, she should know that [if nothing happens to her], *zekhut* is what suspends [the curse from taking effect]."

> R. Simeon says, "*Zekhut* does not suspend the effects of the bitter water.

"And if you say, '*Zekhut* does suspend the effects of the bitter water,' you will weaken the effect of the water for all the women who have to drink it.

"And you give a bad name to all the women who drink it who turned out to be pure.

"For people will say, 'They are unclean, but *zekhut* suspended the effects of the water for them.' "

Rabbi says, "*Zekhut* does suspend the effects of the bitter water. But she will not bear children or continue to be pretty. And she will waste away, and in the end she will have the same [unpleasant] death."

Now if we insert for *zekhut* at each point, "the heritage of virtue and its consequent entitlements," we have good sense. That is to say, the woman may not suffer the penalty to which she is presumably condemnable, not because her act or condition (her innocence) has secured her acquittal, but because she enjoys some advantage extrinsic to her own act or condition. She may be guilty, but she may also possess a benefice deriving by inheritance, hence, heritage of virtue, and so be entitled to a protection because of someone *else's* action or condition.

That meaning may be sustained by the passage at hand, even though it is not required by it; still, it seems plausible that the word *zekhut* in the Mishnah bears not only a juridical but a religious sense. If it does, as I think it does, that usage is not systemically critical, or even very important. If we search the pages of the Mishnah for places in which the conception in hand is present without the word *zekhut,* we find none—not one. For example, there simply is no reference to gaining *zekhut* through doing one's duty, as in reciting the *Shema* or studying the Torah, and references to studying the Torah, such as at Mishnah *Peah* 1:1, do not encompass the conception that, in doing so, one gains an entitlement either for one's own descendants or for all Israel. On that basis we are on firm ground in holding the twin positions that (1) the word bore the important one of all its meanings later on, and (2) in the philosophical system adumbrated by the Mishnah, the word played no systemic role commensurate with the importance accorded to it and its sense in the religious system that took shape in the successor writings.

The evidence of tractate *Avot* is consistent with that of the

Mishnah. The juridical sense of *zekhut* occurs at 1:6, "Judge everybody as though to be acquitted," more comprehensibly translated, "And give everybody the benefit of the doubt," forming a reasonably coherent statement with the usages important in Mishnah *Sanhedrin*. In *Avot*, however, we have clear evidence for the sense of the word that seems to be demanded later on.

Avot 2:2

"And all who work with the community—let them work with them for the sake of Heaven.

"For the [1] *zekhut* of their fathers strengthens them, and their [fathers'] [2] righteousness stands forever.

"And as for you, I credit you with a great reward, as if you had done [all of the work required by the community on your own merit alone]."

Here there is no meaning possible other than the one I have given above: "the heritage of virtue and its consequent entitlements." The reference to an advantage that one gains by reason of inheritance out of one's fathers' righteousness is demanded by the parallel between *zekhut* of clause 1 and *righteousness* of clause 2. Whatever the conceivable ambiguity of the Mishnah, none is sustained by the context at hand, which is explicit in language and pellucid in message. That the sense is exactly the same as the one I have proposed is shown at the following passages, which seem to exhibit none of the ambiguity that characterized the usage of *zekhut* in the Mishnah:

Avot 5:18

He who causes *zekhut* to the community never causes sin.

And he who causes the community to sin—they never give him a sufficient chance to attain penitence.

Here the contrast is between causing *zekhut* and causing sin, so *zekhut* is the opposite of sin. The continuation is equally clear that a person attained *zekhut* and endowed the community with *zekhut*, or sinned and made the community sin:

Moses attained *zekhut* and bestowed *zekhut* on the community.

So the *zekhut* of the community is assigned to his [credit],

    as it is said, "He executed the justice of the Lord and his judgments with Israel" (Deuteronomy 33:21).

Jeroboam sinned and caused the community to sin.

So the sin of the community is assigned to his [debit],

    as it is said, "For the sins of Jeroboam which he committed and wherewith he made Israel to sin" (1 Kings 15:30).

The appropriateness of interpreting the passage in the way I have proposed will now be evident. All that is required is to substitute for *zekhut* the proposed translation:

Moses attained *the heritage of virtue* and bestowed *its consequent entitlements* on the community.

So the *heritage of virtue and its entitlements* enjoyed by the community are assigned to his [credit]. . . .

The sense then is simple. Moses, through unspecified actions of his own, acquired *zekhut*, which is the credit for such actions that bestowed upon him certain supernatural entitlements; and he passed on as an inheritance that credit, a lien on Heaven for the performance of these supernatural entitlements: *zekhut*, pure and simple.

If we may now define *zekhut* as the initial system explicated in tractate *Avot* has used the word, we must pay close attention to the antonymic structure before us. The juridical opposites are *guilty* as against *innocent*, and the religious opposites, as we have now seen, are *sin* as against the *opposite* of sin. That seems to me to require our interpreting *zekhut* as (1) an action, as distinct from a (mere) attitude, that (2) is precisely the opposite of a sinful one; it is, moreover, an action that (3) may be done by an individual or by the community at large, and one that (4) a leader may provoke the community to do (or not do).

The contrast of sin to *zekhut* requires further attention. Since, in general, two classes that are compared to begin with, if different, must constitute opposites, the ultimate definition of *zekhut* requires us to ask how *zekhut* is precisely the opposite of sin. For one thing, as we recall, Scripture is explicit that the burden of sins cannot be

passively inherited willy-nilly, but, to form a heritage of guilt, must
be actively accepted and renewed; the children cannot be made to
suffer for the sins of the parents, unless they repeat them. Then
zekhut, being a mirror image, can be passively inherited, not by
one's own merit[3] but by one's good fortune alone. But what
constitutes these *actions* that form mirror images of sins? Answers to
that critical question must emerge from the systemic documents
before us, since they do not occur in those of the initial system.

That simple fact, too, attests to the systemic centrality of *zekhut:*
it defines a principal point of exegesis. For the question left open by
the Mishnah's merely episodic and somewhat opaque reference to
the matter, and the incomplete evidence provided by its principal
apologetic's representation as well, alas, is the critical issue. Precisely
which actions generate *zekhut,* and which do not? To find answers
to those questions, we have to turn to the successor documents,
since not a single passage in the Mishnah or tractate *Avot* provides
me with information on the matter of what I must do to secure for
myself or my descendants a lien upon Heaven, that is, an entitlement to supernatural favor and even action of a miraculous order.

We turn first to the conception of the *zekhut* that has been
accumulated by the patriarchs and been passed on to Israel, their
children. The reason is that the single distinctive trait of *zekhut,* as
we have seen it to this point, is its transitive quality: one need not
earn the supernatural power and resource represented by the things
you can do if you have *zekhut.* One can inherit that entitlement

---

[3]Indeed, the conception of merit is so alien to the concept of *zekhut,* which one
enjoys whether or not one personally has done something to merit it, that I am
puzzled as to how "merit" ever seemed to anyone to serve as a translation of the
word *zekhut.* If I can inherit the entitlements accrued by my ancestors, then these
entitlements not only cannot be classed as merit(ed by me), they must be classed
as a heritage bestowed by others. Along these same lines, the *zekhut* that I gain for
myself may entitle me to certain benefits, but it may also accrue to the advantage
of the community in which I live (as is made explicit by *Avot* for Moses's *zekhut*)
and also to that of my descendants. The transitive character of *zekhut,* the power
we have of receiving it from others and handing it on to others, serves as the
distinctive trait of this particular entitlement, and, it must follow, *zekhut* is the
opposite of merit and its character is obscured by the confusion created through
that long-standing but wrong translation of the word.

from others, dead or living. Moses not only attains *zekhut* but he also imparts it to the community of which he is leader, and the same is so for any Israelite. That conception is broadened in the successor documents into the deeply historical notion of *zekhut avot*, empowerment of a supernatural character to which Israel is entitled by reason of what the patriarchs and matriarchs did long ago. That conception forms the foundation for the paramount sense of *zekhut* in the successor system: Israel possesses a lien upon Heaven by reason of God's love for the patriarchs and matriarchs and his appreciation for certain things they did. *Zekhut*, as we noted earlier, explains the present—particularly what is odd and unpredictable in it—by appeal to the past, hence forms a distinctively historical conception.

Within the historically grounded metaphor of Israel as a family expressed by the conception of *zekhut avot*, Israel was a family, the children of Abraham, Isaac, and Jacob, or children of Israel, in a concrete and genealogical sense. Israel hence fell into the genus *family*, as the particular species of family generated by Abraham and Sarah. The distinguishing trait of that species was that it possessed the heritage of the patriarchs and matriarchs, and that inheritance, consisting of *zekhut*, served as protection and support. It follows that the systemic position of the conception of *zekhut* to begin with lies in its power to define the social entity, and hence *zekhut* (in the terms of the initial category formation, the philosophical one) forms a fundamentally political conception[4] and only secondarily an economic and philosophical one.

---

[4]That political definition of the systemic role and function of *zekhut* is strengthened by the polemical power of the concept vis-à-vis the Christian critique of Israel after the flesh. The doctrine of the *zekhut* of the ancestors served as a component of the powerful polemic concerning Israel. Specifically, that concrete, historical Israel, meaning for Christian theologians "Israel after the flesh," in the literature before us manifestly and explicitly claimed fleshly origin in Abraham and Sarah. The extended family indeed constituted precisely what the Christian theologians said: an Israel after the flesh, a family linked by genealogy. The heritage then became an inheritance, and what was inherited from the ancestors was a heavenly store, a treasure of *zekhut*, which protected the descendants when their own *zekhut* proved insufficient. The conflict is a political one, involving the legitimacy of the power of the now-Christian empire, denied by this "Israel," affirmed by the other one.

But *zekhut* serves, in particular, that counterpart category that speaks of not legitimate but illegitimate violence, not power but weakness. In context, time and again, we observe that *zekhut* is the power of the weak: people who through their own capacity can accomplish nothing, but through what others do for them in leaving a heritage of *zekhut* can accomplish miracles. And, not to miss the stunning message of the triplet of stories cited above, *zekhut* also is what the weak and excluded and despised can do that outweighs in power what the great masters of the Torah have accomplished. In the context of a system that represents Torah as supernatural, that claim of priority for *zekhut* represents a considerable transvaluation of power. Furthermore, *zekhut* forms the inheritance of the disinherited: what you receive as a heritage when you have nothing in the present and have gotten nothing in the past, that scarce resource that is free and unearned but much valued. So let us dwell upon the definitive character of the transferability of *zekhut* in its formulation, *zekhut avot*, the *zekhut* handed on by the ancestors, the transitive character of the concept of a heritage of entitlements.

It is in the successor documents that the concept of *zekhut* is joined with *avot*, that is, left by the ancestors, as Israel's inheritance, yielding the very specific notion of Israel not as a (mere) community (as in tractate *Avot*'s reference to Moses' bestowing *zekhut* upon the community) but as a family with a history that takes the form of a genealogy, as represented in Genesis. Now *zekhut* was joined to the metaphor of that genealogy and served to form the missing link, explaining how the inheritance and heritage were transmitted from the ancestors to their heirs. Consequently, the family, called "Israel," could draw upon the family estate, the inherited *zekhut*, in such a way as to benefit from the heritage of yesterday. This notion involved very concrete problems. If "Israel, the family" sinned, it could call upon the *zekhut* accumulated by Abraham and Isaac at the binding of Isaac (Genesis 22) to win forgiveness for that sin. True, "fathers will not die on account of the sin of the sons," but the children may benefit from the *zekhut* of the forebears. That concrete expression of the larger metaphor imparted to the metaphor a practical consequence, moral and theological, that was not at all neglected.

A survey of *Genesis Rabbah* proves indicative of the character and use of the doctrine of *zekhut,* because that systematic reading of the book of Genesis dealt with the founders of the family and made explicit the definition of Israel as family. What we shall see is that *zekhut* draws in its wake the notion of the inheritance of the ongoing (historical) family of Abraham and Sarah, and *zekhut* worked itself out in the moments of crisis of that family in its larger affairs. That conception comes to expression in what follows:

Genesis Rabbah LXXVI:V

". . . for with only my staff I crossed this Jordan, and now I have become two companies":

R. Judah bar Simon in the name of R. Yohanan: "In the Torah, in the Prophets, and in the Writings we find proof that the Israelites were able to cross the Jordan only on account of the *zekhut* achieved by Jacob:

"In the Torah: '. . . for with only my staff I crossed this Jordan, and now I have become two companies.'

"In the prophets: 'Then you shall let your children know, saying, "Israel came over this Jordan on dry land" ' (Joshua 4:22), meaning our father, Israel.

"In the Writings: 'What ails you, O you sea, that you flee? You Jordan, that you burn backward? At the presence of the God of Jacob' (Psalms 114:5*ff.*)."

Here is a perfect illustration of my definition of *zekhut* as an entitlement I enjoy by reason of what someone else—an ancestor— has done, an entitlement involving supernatural power. Jacob did not only leave *zekhut* as an estate to his heirs. The process is reciprocal and ongoing. *Zekhut* deriving from the ancestors had helped Jacob himself:

Genesis Rabbah LXXVII:III.3

"When the man saw that he did not prevail against Jacob, [he touched the hollow of his thigh, and Jacob's thigh was put out of joint as he wrestled with him]" (Genesis 32:25):

Said R. Hinena bar Isaac, "[God said to the angel,] 'He is coming against you with five "amulets" hung on his neck, that is, his own *zekhut*, the *zekhut* of his father and of his mother and of his grandfather and of his grandmother.

" 'Check yourself out, can you stand up against even his own *zekhut* [let alone the *zekhut* of his parents and grandparents].'

"The matter may be compared to a king who had a savage dog and a tame lion. The king would take his son and sic him against the lion, and if the dog came to have a fight with the son, he would say to the dog, 'The lion cannot have a fight with him, are you going to make out in a fight with him?'

"So if the nations come to have a fight with Israel, the Holy One, blessed be he, says to them, 'Your angelic prince could not stand up to Israel, and as to you, how much the more so!' "

The collectivity of *zekhut*, not only its transferability, is illustrated here: what an individual does confers *zekhut* on the social entity. Moreover, it involves the legitimate exercise of supernatural power, and the reciprocity of the process is extended in all directions. Accordingly, what we have is first and foremost the exercise of legitimate violence, hence a political power.

Zekhut might project not only backward, but forward as well. Thus Joseph accrued so much *zekhut* that the generations that came before him were credited with his *zekhut*:

Genesis Rabbah LXXXIV:V.2

"These are the generations of the family of Jacob. Joseph [being seventeen years old, was shepherding the flock with his brothers]" (Genesis 37:2):

These generations came along only on account of the *zekhut* of Joseph.

Did Jacob go to Laban for any reason other than for Rachel?

These generations thus waited until Joseph was born, in line with this verse: "And when Rachel had borne Joseph, Jacob said to Laban, 'Send me away' " (Genesis 30:25).

Who brought them down to Egypt? It was Joseph.

Who supported them in Egypt? It was Joseph.

The sea split open only on account of the *zekhut* of Joseph: "The waters saw you, O God" (Psalms 77:17). "You have with your arm redeemed your people, the sons of Jacob and Joseph" (Psalms 77:16).

R. Yudan said, "Also the Jordan was divided only on account of the *zekhut* of Joseph."

The passage at hand asks why only Joseph is mentioned as the family of Jacob. The inner polemic is that the *zekhut* of Jacob and Joseph would more than suffice to overcome Esau. Not only so, but Joseph survived because of the *zekhut* of his ancestors:

Genesis Rabbah LXXXVII:VIII.1

"She caught him by his garment . . . but he left his garment in her hand and fled and got out of the house. [And when she saw that he had left his garment in her hand and had fled out of the house, she called to the men of her household and said to them, 'See he has brought among us a Hebrew to insult us; he came in to me to lie with me, and I cried out with a loud voice, and when he heard that I lifted up my voice and cried, he left his garment with me and fled and got out of the house']" (Genesis 39:13–15):

He escaped through the *zekhut* of the fathers, in line with this verse: "And he brought him forth outside" (Genesis 15:5).

Simeon of Qitron said, "It was on account of bringing up the bones of Joseph that the sea was split: 'The sea saw it and fled' (Psalms 114:3), on the *zekhut* of this: '. . . and fled and got out.' "

Zekhut, we see, is both personal and national, the second paragraph above referring to Joseph's enjoying the *zekhut* he had inherited and the third referring to Israel's enjoying the *zekhut* they gained through their supererogatory loyalty to that same *zekhut*-rich personality. How do we know that the *zekhut* left as a heritage by ancestors is in play? Here is an explicit, textual answer:

Genesis Rabbah LXXIV:XII.1

"If the God of my father, the God of Abraham and the Fear of Isaac, had not been on my side, surely now you would have sent me away empty-handed. God saw my affliction and the labor of my hand and rebuked you last night" (Genesis 31:41–42):

Zebedee b. Levi and R. Joshua b. Levi:

Zebedee said, "Every passage in which reference is made to 'if' tells of an appeal to the *zekhut* accrued by the patriarchs."

Said to him R. Joshua, "But it is written, 'Except we had lingered' (Genesis 43:10) [a passage not related to the *zekhut* of the patriarchs]."

He said to him, "They themselves would not have come up except for the *zekhut* of the patriarchs, for it if it were not for the *zekhut* of the patriarchs, they never would have been able to go up from there in peace."

The issue of the *zekhut* of the patriarchs comes up in the reference to the God of the fathers. The conception of the *zekhut* of the patriarchs is explicit, not general. It specifies what later benefit to the heir, Israel the family, derived from which particular action of a patriarch or matriarch.

Genesis Rabbah XLIII:VIII.2-3

"And Abram gave him a tenth of everything" (Genesis 14:20):

R. Judah in the name of R. Nehorai: "On the strength of that blessing the three great pegs on which the world depends, Abraham, Isaac, and Jacob, derived sustenance.

"Abraham: 'And the Lord blessed Abraham in *all* things' (Genesis 24:1) on account of the *zekhut* that 'he gave him a tenth of *all* things' (Genesis 14:20).

"Isaac: 'And I have eaten of *all* (Genesis 27:33), on account of the *zekhut* that 'he gave him a tenth of *all* things' (Genesis 14:20).

"Jacob: 'Because God has dealt graciously with me and because I have all' (Genesis 33:11) on account of the *zekhut* that 'he gave him a tenth of *all* things' (Genesis 14:20).

Whence did Israel gain the *zekhut* of receiving the blessing of the priests?

R. Judah said, "It was from Abraham: '*So* shall your seed be' (Genesis 15:5), while it is written in connection with the priestly blessing: '*So* shall you bless the children of Israel' (Numbers 6:23)."

R. Nehemiah said, "It was from Isaac: 'And I and the lad will go *so* far' (Genesis 22:5), therefore said the Holy One, blessed be he, '*So* shall you bless the children of Israel' (Numbers 6:23)."

And rabbis say, "It was from Jacob: '*So* shall you say to the house of Jacob' (Exodus 19:3) (in line with the statement, '*So* shall you bless the children of Israel' (Numbers 6:23)."

The picture is clear. "Israel" constitutes a family as a genealogical and juridical fact. It inherits the estate of the ancestors. It hands on that estate. It lives by the example of the matriarchs and patriarchs, and its history exemplifies events in their lives. And *zekhut* forms that entitlement that one generation may transmit to the next, in a way in which the heritage of sin is not to be transmitted except by reason of the deeds of the successor generation. The good that one does lives onward, the evil is interred with the bones.

Zekhut thus not only describes our relationship with God and the character of God but also sets forth the meaning of historical existence, that is, the *zekhut avot*. Let me present a statement of the legitimate power, sufficient to achieve salvation, which in this context always bears a political dimension, imparted by the *zekhut* of the ancestors. That *zekhut* will enable them to accomplish the political goals of Israel: its attaining self-rule and avoiding government by Gentiles. This statement appeals to the binding of Isaac as the source of the *zekhut*, which will in the end lead to the salvation of Israel. What is important here is that the *zekhut* that is inherited joins together with the *zekhut* of one's own deeds; one inherits the *zekhut* of the past and, moreover, if one does what the progenitors did, one in addition secures an entitlement on one's own account. So the difference between *zekhut* and sin lies in the sole issue of transmissibility:

Genesis Rabbah LVI:II

Said R. Isaac, "And all was on account of the *zekhut* attained by the act of prostration.

"Abraham returned in peace from Mount Moriah only on account of the *zekhut* owing to the act of prostration: '. . . and we will worship [through an act of prostration] and come [then, on that account] again to you' (Genesis 22:5).

"The Israelites were redeemed only on account of the *zekhut* owing to the act of prostration: 'And the people believed . . . then they bowed their heads and prostrated themselves' (Exodus 4:31).

"The Torah was given only on account of the *zekhut* owing to the act of prostration: 'And worship [prostrate themselves] you afar off' (Exodus 24:1).

"Hannah was remembered only on account of the zekhut owing to the act of prostration: 'And they worshipped before the Lord' (I Samuel 1:19).

"The exiles will be brought back only on account of the zekhut owing to the act of prostration: 'And it shall come to pass in that day that a great horn shall be blown and they shall come that were lost . . . and that were dispersed . . . and they shall worship the Lord in the holy mountain at Jerusalem' (Isaiah 27:13).

"The Temple was built only on account of the zekhut owing to the act of prostration: 'Exalt you the Lord our God and worship at his holy hill' (Psalms 99:9).

"The dead will live only on account of the zekhut owing to the act of prostration: 'Come let us worship and bend the knee, let us kneel before the Lord our maker' (Psalms 95:6)."

The entire history of Israel flows from its acts of worship ("prostration") beginning with that performed by Abraham at the binding of Isaac. Every sort of advantage Israel has ever gained came about through that act of worship done by Abraham and imitated thereafter. The family Israel draws upon that zekhut but, by doing the deeds the ancestors did, it also enhances its heritage and leaves to the descendants greater entitlement than they would enjoy by reason of their own actions. But their own actions—here, prostration in worship—generate zekhut as well.

Accordingly, as I claimed at the outset, zekhut may be personal or inherited. The zekhut deriving from the prior generations is collective and affects all Israel. But one's own deeds can generate zekhut for oneself, so it is equally personal. Specifically, Jacob reflects on the power—the supernatural favor—that Esau's own zekhut had gained for Esau. Jacob then feared that, because of Esau's zekhut, he, Jacob, would not be able to overcome him. Esau's zekhut was a credit gained by his own proper action, an action not required but, if done, one to be rewarded. In Esau's case, it was the simple fact that he had remained in the holy land and honored Isaac:

Genesis Rabbah LXXVI:II

"Then Jacob was greatly afraid and distressed" (Genesis 32:8): [This is Jacob's soliloquy:] "Because of all those years that Esau was living in the

Land of Israel, perhaps he may come against me with the power of the *zekhut* he has now attained by dwelling in the Land of Israel.

"Because of all those years of paying honor to his father, perhaps he may come against me with the power of the *zekhut* he attained by honoring his father.

"So he said: 'Let the days of mourning for my father be at hand, then I will slay my brother Jacob' (Genesis 27:41).

"Now the old man is dead."

The important point, then, is that *zekhut* is not only inherited but also accomplished on one's own behalf. By extension, we recognize, the successor system opens a place for recognition of the individual man or woman as a matter of fact. Thus there is space within the system of *zekhut* for a private person, and the individual is linked to the social order through the shared possibilities of generating or inheriting an entitlement upon Heaven. The philosophical system, by contrast, had regarded as important principally the issue of classifying persons, such as by castes or by other indicators; a system of hierarchical classification treated the individual in the way it treated all other matters, and so, we now see, does the system of *zekhut* now to be broadened into the definition, accomplishing a lien upon Heaven.

For if we now ask what sorts of deeds generate *zekhut,* we realize that those deeds produce a common result of gaining for their doer, and the doer's heirs, an entitlement for Heavenly favor and support when needed. That fact of benefit from *zekhut* brings us to the systemic message to the living generation, its account of what now is to be done. That message proves acutely contemporary, for its stress is on the power of a single action to create sufficient *zekhut* to outweigh a life of sin. Then the contrast between sin and *zekhut* gains greater depth still. One sin of sufficient weight condemns, one act of *zekhut* of sufficient weight saves; the entire issue of entitlements out of the past gives way, then, when we realize what is actually at stake.

We recall that Torah study is one means, but not the only means, for an individual to gain access to that heritage, to get *zekhut.* Furthermore, the merit gained by Torah study is no different from the merit gained by acts of a supererogatory character. If one gets *zekhut* for studying the Torah, then we must suppose there is no holy deed that does not generate its share of *zekhut*. But when it comes to specifying the things one does to get *zekhut,* the documents before us speak of what the Torah does not require but does recommend: not what we are commanded to do in detail, but what the right attitude, formed within the Torah, leads us to do on our own volition:

Yerushalmi Taanit 3:11.IV

There was a house that was about to collapse over there [in Babylonia], and Rab set one of his disciples in the house, until they had cleared out everything from the house. When the disciple left the house, the house collapsed.

And there are those who say that it was R. Adda bar Ahwah.

Sages sent and said to him, "What sort of good deeds are to your credit [that you have that much merit]?"

He said to them, "In my whole life no man ever got to the synagogue in the morning before I did. I never left anybody there when I went out. I never walked four cubits without speaking words of Torah. Nor did I ever mention teachings of Torah in an inappropriate setting. I never laid out a bed and slept for a regular period of time. I never took great strides among the associates. I never called my fellow by a nickname. I never rejoiced in the embarrassment of my fellow. I never cursed my fellow when I was lying by myself in bed. I never walked over in the marketplace to someone who owed me money.

"In my entire life I never lost my temper in my household."

This was meant to carry out that which is stated as follows: "I will give heed to the way that is blameless. Oh when wilt thou come to me? I will walk with integrity of heart within my house" (Psalms 101:2).

What I find striking in this story is that mastery of the Torah is only one means of attaining the merit that enabled the sage to keep the house from collapsing. The question to R. Adda bar Ahwah provides the key, together with its answer. For what the sage did to gain such remarkable merit is not to master such-and-so many tractates of the Mishnah. Nor does the storyteller refer to carrying out the commandments of the Torah as specified. It was rather acts that expressed courtesy, consideration, restraint. These acts, which no specification can encompass in detail, produced the right

attitude, one of gentility, that led to gaining merit. Acts rewarded
with an entitlement to supernatural power are those of self-
abnegation or the avoidance of power over others—not taking great
strides among the associates, not using a nickname, not rejoicing in
the embarrassment of one's fellow, not singling out one's debtor—
and the submission to the will and the requirement of self-esteem of
others.

Here, in a moral setting, we find the politics replicated: the form
of power that the system promises derives from the rejection of
power that the world recognizes—legitimate violence replaced by
legitimation of the absence of the power to commit violence or of
the failure to commit violence. This counterpart politics of not
exercising power over others, moreover, produced that scarcest of
all resources, supernatural favor, by which the holy man could hold
up a tottering building. Here then we find politics and economics
united in the counterpart category formed of *zekhut:* the absence of
power yielding supernatural power, the valuation of the intangible,
Torah, yielding supernatural power. It was, then, that entitlement
to supernatural favor that formed the systemic center.

And what do we have to do to secure an inheritance of *zekhut* for
our heirs? Following is a concrete example of how acts of worth or
zekhut accrue to the benefit of the heirs. What makes it especially
indicative is that here Gentiles have the power to acquire *zekhut* for
their descendants, which is coherent with the system's larger
interest in not only Israel (as against the faceless, undifferentiated
outsider) but the Gentiles as well. Here we see that the successor
system may hold within the orbit of its generative conception also
the history of the Gentiles:

Genesis Rabbah C:VI.1

"When they came to the threshing floor of Atad, which is beyond the
Jordan, they lamented there with a very great and sorrowful lamentation,
and he made a mourning for his father seven days" (Genesis 50:10):
Said R. Samuel bar Nahman, "We have reviewed the entire Scripture
and found no other place called Atad. And can there be a threshing floor
for thorns [the Hebrew word for thorn being *atad*]?

"But this refers to the Canaanites. It teaches that they were worthy of being threshed like thorns. And on account of what *zekhut* were they saved? It was on account of the acts of kindness that they performed for our father, Jacob [on the occasion of the mourning for his death]."

And what were the acts of kindness that they performed for our father, Jacob?

R. Eleazar said, "[When the bier was brought up there,] they unloosened the girdle of their loins."

R. Simeon b. Laqish said, "They untied the shoulder knots."

R. Judah b. R. Shalom said, "They pointed with their fingers and said, 'This is a grievous mourning to the Egyptians' (Genesis 50:11)."

Rabbi said, "They stood upright."

Now is it not an argument a fortiori: now if these, who did not do a thing with their hands or feet, but only because they pointed their fingers, were saved from punishment, Israel, which performs an act of kindness [for the dead] whether they are adults or children, whether with their hands or with their feet, how much the more so [will they enjoy the *zekhut* of being saved from punishment]!

Said R. Abbahu, "Those seventy days that lapsed between the first letter and the second match the seventy days that the Egyptians paid respect to Jacob. [Seventy days elapsed from Haman's letter of destruction until Mordecai's letter announcing the repeal of the decree] (cf. Esther 3:12, 8:9). The latter letter, which permitted the Jews to take vengeance on their would-be destroyers, should have come earlier, but it was delayed seventy days as a reward for the honor shown by the Egyptians to Jacob."

The Egyptians gained *zekhut* by honoring Jacob in his death, so says Abbahu. This same point then registers for the Canaanites. The connection is somewhat farfetched, that is, through the reference to the threshing floor, but the point is a strong one. And the explanation of history extends not only to Israel's, but also to that of the Canaanites.

If the Egyptians and the Canaanites, how much the more so Israelites! What is it that Israelites as a nation do to gain a lien upon Heaven for themselves or entitlements of supernatural favor for their descendants? Here is one representative answer to that question:

Genesis Rabbah LXXIV:XII.1

"If the God of my father, the God of Abraham and the Fear of Isaac, had not been on my side, surely now you would have sent me away empty-handed. God saw my affliction and the labor of my hand and rebuked you last night" (Genesis 31:41–42):

Zebedee b. Levi and R. Joshua b. Levi:

Zebedee said, "Every passage in which reference is made to 'if' tells of an appeal to the *zekhut* accrued by the patriarchs."

Said to him R. Joshua, "But it is written, 'Except we had lingered' (Genesis 43:10) [a passage not related to the *zekhut* of the patriarchs]."

He said to him, "They themselves would not have come up except for the *zekhut* of the patriarchs, for if it were not for the *zekhut* of the patriarchs, they never would have been able to go up from there in peace."

Said R. Tanhuma, "There are those who produce the matter in a different version." [It is given as follows:]

R. Joshua and Zebedee b. Levi:

R. Joshua said, "Every passage in which reference is made to 'if' tells of an appeal to the *zekhut* accrued by the patriarchs except for the present case."

He said to him, "This case too falls under the category of an appeal to the *zekhut* of the patriarchs."

So much for *zekhut* that is inherited from the patriarchs, a now familiar notion. But what about the deeds of Israel in the here and now?

R. Yohanan said, "It was on account of the *zekhut* achieved through sanctification of the divine name."

R. Levi said, "It was on account of the *zekhut* achieved through faith and the *zekhut* achieved through Torah.

Faith despite the here and now, study of the Torah—these are what Israel does in the here and now with the result that they gain an entitlement for themselves or their heirs.

"The *zekhut* achieved through faith: 'If I had not believed . . .' (Psalms 27:13).

"The *zekhut* achieved through Torah: 'Unless your Torah had been my delight' (Psalms 119:92)."

"God saw my affliction and the labor of my hand and rebuked you last night" (Genesis 31:41–42):

Said R. Jeremiah b. Eleazar, "More beloved is hard labor than the *zekhut* achieved by the patriarchs, for the *zekhut* achieved by the patriarchs served to afford protection for property only, while the *zekhut* achieved by hard labor served to afford protection for lives.

"The *zekhut* achieved by the patriarchs served to afford protection for property only: 'If the God of my father, the God of Abraham and the Fear of Isaac, had not been on my side, surely now you would have sent me away empty-handed.'

"The *zekhut* achieved by hard labor served to afford protection for lives: 'God saw my affliction and the labor of my hand and rebuked you last night.' "

Here is as good an account as any of the theology of *zekhut*. The *zekhut* of the patriarchs comes up in the reference to the God of the fathers. This conception is explicit, not general. It specifies what later benefit to the heir, Israel the family, derived from which particular action of a patriarch or matriarch. But acts of faith and Torah study form only one medium; hard labor, that is, devotion to one's calling, defines that source of *zekhut* that is going to be accessible to those many Israelites unlikely to distinguish themselves either by Torah study and acts of faith, encompassing the sanctification of God's name, or by acts of amazing gentility and restraint.

Zekhut therefore defines the structure of the entire cosmic social order and explains how it is supposed to function. It is the encompassing quality of *zekhut*, its pertinence to Jew and Gentile, past and present and future, high and low, rich and poor, gifted and ordinary, that marks its message as the systemic statement, now fully revealed as the conception of reciprocal response between Heaven and Israel on earth, to acts of devotion beyond the requirements of the Torah but defined all the same by the Torah. As Scripture had said, God responds to the faith of the ancient generations by supernatural acts to which, on their own account, the moderns are not entitled, hence a heritage of entitlement. But those acts, now fully defined for us, can and ought to be done also by the living generation, and, as a matter of fact, there is none today, at the time of the system builders, exempt from the systemic message and its demands: even steadfastness in accomplishing the humble work of the everyday and the here and now.

The systemic statement made by the usages of *zekhut* speaks of relationship, function, the interplay of humanity and God. One's store of *zekhut* derives from a relationship, that is, from one's forebears. That is one dimension of the relationships in which one stands. *Zekhut* also forms a measure of one's own relationship with Heaven, a fact attested to by the power of one person, but not another, to pray and so bring rain. What sort of relationship does *zekhut*, as the opposite of sin, then posit? It is not one of coercion, for Heaven cannot force us to do those types of deeds that yield *zekhut*, and, as story after story suggests, what generates *zekhut* is doing what we ought to do but do not have to do. But then, we cannot coerce Heaven to do what we want done either, for example, it is obligatory to carry out the commandments, but doing so does not obligate Heaven.

Whence then our lien on Heaven? It is through deeds of a supererogatory character, to which Heaven responds by deeds of a supererogatory character: supernatural favor to this one, who through deeds of ingratiation of the other or self-abnegation or restraint exhibits the attitude that in Heaven precipitates a counterpart attitude, hence generating *zekhut*. The simple fact that rabbis cannot pray and bring rain but a simple ass driver can tells the whole story. The relationship measured by *zekhut* contains an element of unpredictability for which appeal to the *zekhut* inherited from ancestors accounts. So while I cannot coerce Heaven, I can through *zekhut* gain acts of favor from Heaven, and that is by doing what Heaven cannot require of me.

This is what it means to love God with all one's heart, soul, and mind, but it also tells us what the sages understand God to be. Heaven responds to my attitude in carrying out my duties—and more than my duties. That act of pure disinterest—giving the woman my means of livelihood—is the one that gains for me Heaven's deepest interest. What that tells us about God is that our God is a God of love, and love is always specific and is never bound by rules. That is what makes love love. *Zekhut* is the power of the powerless, the riches of the disinherited, the valuation and valorization of the will of those who have no right to will. What has this to do with God? These—the weak and disinherited, the street people of the ages—are the very opposite of God; they form the mirror image of God, and they realize what it means to be "in our image, after our likeness."

PART III

The Talmud of Babylonia and God's Personality

6

The God We See
and Know and Love

Our present conception that humanity "in our image" is the mirror image of God was not the view of our sages of blessed memory. Their view was that God and humanity are indistinguishable in their physical traits. They are distinguished, however, in other, important ways. The issue of the Talmud of Babylonia is the re-presentation of God in the form of humanity, but as God. Let us begin with the conception that God and the human being are mirror images of one another. Here in Genesis *Rabbah* we find the simple claim that the angels could not discern any physical difference whatever between man—Adam—and God:

Genesis Rabbah VIII:X

Said R. Hoshaiah, "When the Holy One, blessed be he, came to create the first man, the ministering angels mistook him [for God, since man was in God's image,] and wanted to say before him, 'Holy, [holy, holy is the Lord of hosts].'

"To what may the matter be compared? To the case of a king and a governor who were set in a chariot, and the provincials wanted to greet the king, "Sovereign!" But they did not know which one of them was which. What did the king do? He turned the governor out and put him away from the chariot, so that people would know who was king.

"So too when the Holy One, blessed be he, created the first man, the angels mistook him [for God]. What did the Holy One, blessed be he, do? He put him to sleep, so everyone knew that he was a mere man.

"That is in line with the following verse of Scripture: 'Cease you from man, in whose nostrils is a breath, for how little is he to be accounted' (Isaiah 2:22)."

It was in the Talmud of Babylonia in particular that God is represented as a fully exposed personality, like man. There we see in a variety of dimensions the single characterization of God as a personality that we can know and love.

Telling stories—as in Hasidism later on—provides the particular means by which theological traits that generations had long affirmed are now portrayed as qualities of the personality of God, who is like a human being. It is one thing to hypostatize a theological abstraction, for example, "The quality of mercy said before the Holy One, blessed be he. . . ." It is quite another to construct a conversation between God and, let us say, David, with a complete argument and a rich interchange, in which God's merciful character is spelled out as the trait of a specific personality. And that is what we find in the Bavli and, so far as my survey suggests, not in any prior document.

Specifically, it is in the Bavli that the specification of an attribute of God, such as being long-suffering, is restated by means of narrative. God emerges not as an abstract entity with theological traits but as a fully exposed personality. God is portrayed as engaged in conversation with human beings because God and humanity can understand one another within the same rules of discourse. When we speak of the personality of God, we shall see, traits of a corporeal, emotional, and social character form the repertoire of appropriate characteristics. To begin with, we will consider the particular means by which these traits are set forth in the pages of the Talmud of Babylonia (or Bavli).

The following story shows us the movement from the abstract and theological to the concrete and narrative mode of discourse about God:

Bavli Sanhedrin III A-B

"And Moses made haste and bowed his head toward the earth and worshipped" (Exodus 34:8)

What did Moses see?

R. Hanina b. Gamula said, "He saw [God's attribute of] being long-suffering [Exodus 34:7]."

Rabbis say, "He saw [the attribute of] truth [Exodus 34:7]. "It has been taught on Tannaite authority in accord with him who has said, "He saw God's attribute of being long-suffering."

For it has been taught on Tannaite authority:

When Moses went up on high, he found the Holy One, blessed be he, sitting and writing, "Long-suffering."

He said to him, "Lord of the world, 'Long-suffering for the righteous?' "

He said to him, "Also for the wicked."

[Moses] said to him, "Let the wicked perish."

He said to him, "Now you will see what you want."

When the Israelites sinned, he said to him, "Did I not say to you, 'Long suffering for the righteous'?"

He said to him, "Lord of the world, did I not say to you, 'Also for the wicked'?"

That is in line with what is written, "And now I beseech you, let the power of my Lord be great, according as you have spoken, saying" (Numbers 14:17).[1]

The statement at the outset is then repeated in narrative form. Once we are told that God is long-suffering, it is in particular, narrative form that that trait is given definition. God then emerges as a personality, specifically because Moses engages in argument with God. He reproaches God, questions God's actions and judgments, holds God to a standard of consistency—and receives appropriate responses. God in heaven does not argue with humanity on earth. God in heaven issues decrees, forms the premise of the earthly rules, constitutes a presence, may even take the form of a "you" for hearing and answering prayers.

When God argues, discusses, defends and explains actions, emerges as a personality etched in words, then God attains that personality that imparts to God the status of a being consubstantial with humanity. It is in particular through narrative that that transformation of God from person to personality takes place. Since personality, as I have defined matters, involves physical traits, attitudes of mind, emotion, and intellect consubstantial with those of human beings, and the doing of the deeds people do in the way in which they do them, I have now to demonstrate that all three modes of personality come to full expression in the Bavli. This we

---

[1] [Freedman, *The Babylonian Talmud. Sanhedrin,* p. 764, n. 7: What called forth Moses' worship of God when Israel sinned through the Golden Calf was his vision of the Almighty as long-suffering.]

will do in sequence, ending with a clear demonstration that God
incarnate takes the particular form of a sage.

The claim that the character of God is shaped in the model of a
human being requires substantiation, first of all, in physical traits,
such as are taken for granted in the passage just cited. Incarnation
means precisely that: representation of God in the flesh, as a human
being, in the present context, as a man. We begin with a clear
statement that has God represented as a man, seen in the interpretation of the vision of the prophet Zechariah:

Bavli Sanhedrin 1:1.xlii

And said R. Yohanan, "What is the meaning of the verse of Scripture,
'I saw by night, and behold a man riding upon a red horse, and he stood
among the myrtle trees that were in the bottom' (Zechariah 1:8).?

"What is the meaning of, 'I saw by night'?

"The Holy One blessed be he, sought to turn the entire world into
night.

" 'And behold, a man riding'—'man' refers only to the Holy One,
blessed be he, as it is said, 'The Lord is a man of war, the Lord is his name'
(Exodus 15:3).

" 'On a red horse'—the Holy One, blessed be he, sought to turn the
entire world to blood.

"When, however, he saw Hananiah, Mishael, and Azariah, he cooled
off, as it is said, 'And he stood among the myrtle trees that were in the
deep.' "

We recall the explicit statement in this same regard.

Bavli Berakhot 7A, lvi

[it was necessary for] the Holy One, blessed be he, to say to them, "You
see me in many forms. But I am the same one who was at the sea, I am the
same one who was at Sinai, *I [anokhi] am the Lord your God who brought you
out of the land of Egypt* (Exodus 20:2)."

Scripture of course knows that God has a face, upon which human
beings are not permitted to gaze. But was that face understood in a
physical way, and did God enjoy other physical characteristics? An
affirmative answer clearly emerges in the following:

"And he said, 'You cannot see my face' " (Exodus 33:20).

It was taught on Tannaite authority in the name of R. Joshua b. Qorha, "This is what the Holy One, blessed be he, said to Moses:

" 'When I wanted [you to see my face], you did not want to, now that you want to see my face, I do not want you to.' "

This differs from what R. Samuel bar Nahmani said R. Jonathan said.

For R. Samuel bar Nahmani said R. Jonathan said, "As a reward for three things he received the merit of three things.

"As a reward for: 'And Moses hid his face,' (Exodus 3:6), he had the merit of having a glistening face.

"As a reward for: 'Because he was afraid to' (Exodus 3:6), he had the merit that 'They were afraid to come near him' (Exodus 34:30).

"As a reward for: 'To look upon God' (Exodus 3:6), he had the merit: 'The similitude of the Lord does he behold' (Numbers 12:8)."

"And I shall remove my hand and you shall see my back" (Exodus 33:23).

Said R. Hana bar Bizna R. Simeon the Pious said, "This teaches that the Holy One, blessed be he, showed Moses [how to tie] the knot of the phylacteries."

Bavli Ketubot 111B

That God is able to tie the knot indicates that God has fingers and other physical gifts. God furthermore is portrayed as wearing phylacteries. It follows that God has an arm and a forehead. There is no element of a figurative reading of the indicated traits. That is why, when God is further represented as having eyes and teeth, we have no reason to assign that picture to the status of (mere) poetry:

"His eyes shall be red with wine, and his teeth white with milk" (Genesis 49:12):

R. Dimi, when he came, interpreted the verse in this way: "The congregation of Israel said to the Holy One, blessed be he, 'Lord of the Universe, wink to me with your eyes, which gesture will be sweeter than wine, and show me your teeth, which gesture will be sweeter than milk.' "

The attribution of physical traits is explicit and no longer general or possibly figurative. Another such representation assigns to God cheeks.

Bavli Shabbat 88B

R. Joshua b. Levi, "What is the meaning of the verse, 'His cheeks are as a bed of spices' (Song of Songs 5:13)?

"At every act of speech which went forth from the mouth of the Holy One, blessed be he, the entire world was filled with the fragrance of spices.

"But since at the first act of speech, the world was filled, where did the second act of speech go?

"Along came a strong wind, which removed the first draft of fragrance in sequence."

From eyes and teeth and cheeks, we move on to the physical attributes of having arms and the like. In the following passage, God is given hands and palms.

Bavli Taanit

Further, [the congregation of Israel] made its request in an improper manner, "O God, set me as a seal on your heart, as a seal on your arm" (Song of Songs 8:6).

[But the Holy One, blessed be he, responded in a proper way.] Said the Holy One, blessed be he, to [the congregation of Israel,] "My daughter, now you are asking for something which sometimes can be seen and sometimes cannot be seen. But I shall give you something which can always be seen.

"For it is said, 'Behold, I have graven you on the palms of my hands' (Isaiah 49:16) [and the palms are always visible, in a way in which the heart and arm are not]."

Hands are attached to arms, and it is implicit that God has arms as well. That this is so is shown by the claim that God puts on phylacteries just as Moses does.

Bavli Berakhot 6A, xxxviii

Said R. Abin bar Ada said R. Isaac, "How do we know on the basis of Scripture that the Holy One, blessed be he, puts on phylacteries? As it is said, 'The Lord has sworn by his right hand, and by the arm of his strength' " (Isaiah 62:8).

" 'By his right hand' refers to Torah, as it is said, 'At his right hand was
a fiery law for them' (Deuteronomy 33:2).

" 'And by the arm of his strength' refers to phylacteries, as it is said,
'The Lord will give strength to his people' (Psalms 29:11).

"And how do we know that phylacteries are a strength for Israel? For it
is written, 'And all the peoples of the earth shall see that the name of the
Lord is called upon you and they shall be afraid of you' (Deuteronomy
28:10)."

And it has been taught on Tannaite authority:

R. Eliezer the Great says, "This [Deuteronomy 28:10] refers to the
phylacteries that are put on the head."

Once more we find clear evidence of a corporeal conception of God.
We have no basis on which to assume the authorship at hand meant
a (merely) poetic characterization, or, indeed, what such a more
spiritual interpretation would have required. Assuming that the
words mean precisely what they say, we have to conclude that God
is here portrayed as incarnate. Later on we shall be told what
passages of Scripture are written in the phylacteries that God puts
onto his right arm and forehead.

We shall presently review the range of God's emotions, which
appear to be pretty much the same as human ones. First, however,
let us skip to the matter of God's doing what people do, in the way
in which they do them. In the Bavli's stories God not only looks
like a human being but also does the acts that human beings do. For
example, God spends the day much as does a mortal ruler of Israel,
at least as sages imagine such a figure. That is, he studies the Torah,
makes practical decisions, and sustains the world (meaning, admin-
isters public funds for public needs)—just as (in sages' picture of
themselves) sages do. What gives us a deeply human God is that for
the final part of the day, God plays with his pet, leviathan. Some
correct that view and hold that God spends the rest of the day
teaching youngsters. In passages such as these we therefore see the
concrete expression of a process of the personality of God.

Abodah Zarah

Said R. Judah said Rab, "The day is twelve hours long. During the first
three, the Holy One, blessed be he, is engaged in the study of the Torah.

"During the next three God sits in judgment on the world and when he sees the world sufficiently guilty to deserve destruction, he moves from the seat of justice to the seat of mercy.

"During the third he feeds the whole world, from the horned buffalo to vermin.

"During the fourth he plays with the leviathan, as it is said, 'There is leviathan, whom you have made to play with' (Psalms 104:26)."

[Another authority denies this final point and says,] "What then does God do in the fourth quarter of the day?

"He sits and teaches school children, as it is said, 'Whom shall one teach knowledge, and whom shall one make to understand the message? Those who are weaned from milk' (Isaiah 28:9)."

And what does God do by night?

If you like, I shall propose that he does what he does in daytime.

Or if you prefer: he rides a light cherub and floats in eighteen thousand worlds. . . .

Or if you prefer: he sits and listens to the song of the heavenly creatures, as it is said, "By the day the Lord will command his lovingkindness and in the night his song shall be with me" (Psalms 42:9).

Other actions of God that presuppose a physical capacity are indicated in the following, although the picture is not so clearly one of concrete physical actions as in the earlier instances.

Bavli Baba Mesia 86B

Said R. Judah said Rab, "Everything that Abraham personally did for the ministering angels the Holy One, blessed be he, personally did for his children, and everything that Abraham did through servants the Holy One, blessed be he, carried out also through ministering angels.

" 'And Abraham ran to the herd' (Genesis 18:7). 'And a wind went forth from the Lord' (Numbers 11:31).

" 'And he took butter and milk' (Genesis 18:8). 'Behold, I will rain bread from heaven for you' (Exodus 16:4).

" 'And he stood by them under the tree' (Genesis 18:8). 'Behold, I will stand before you there upon the rock' (Exodus 17:6)."

The passage proceeds to point out further examples of the same parallels. The various actions of God in favor of Israel correspond to the concrete actions of Abraham for God or the angels. This comparison of Abraham's actions to those of God invites the notion that God is represented as incarnate. But in this instance we are not compelled to a reading of God as an essentially corporeal being. The actions God does can be accomplished in some less material or physical way. In the balance, however, we do find evidence to suggest that the authorship of the Bavli understood that God looks like a human being, specifically like a man, and that God does what human beings of a particular order of class do.

The personality of God encompassed not only physical, but also emotional or attitudinal traits. In the final stage of the Judaism of the Dual Torah God emerged as a fully exposed personality. The character of divinity, therefore, encompassed God's virtue, the specific traits of character and personality that God exhibited above and here below. Above all, humility—the virtue that sages most often asked of themselves—characterized the divinity. God wanted people to be humble, and God therefore showed humility.

Bavli Shabbat 89A

Said R. Joshua b. Levi, "When Moses came down from before the Holy One, blessed be he, Satan came and asked [God], 'Lord of the world, Where is the Torah?'

"He said to him, 'I have given it to the earth . . .' [Satan ultimately was told by God to look for the Torah by finding the son of Amram.]

"He went to Moses and asked him, 'Where is the Torah which the Holy One, blessed be he, gave you?'

"He said to him, 'Who am I that the Holy One, blessed be he, should give me the Torah?'

"Said the Holy One, blessed be he, to Moses, 'Moses, you are a liar!'

"He said to him, 'Lord of the world, you have a treasure in store which you have enjoyed every day. Shall I keep it to myself?'

"He said to him, 'Moses, since you have acted with humility, it will bear your name: "Remember the Torah of Moses, my servant" (Malachi 3:22).' "

God here is represented as favoring humility and rewarding the humble with honor. What is important is that God does not here cite Scripture or merely paraphrase it; the conversation is an exchange between two vivid personalities. True enough, Moses, not God, is the hero, but the personality of God emerges in a vivid way. The following passage shows how traits imputed to God also define proper conduct for sages, not to mention other human beings.

At issue once again is humility, and, as we see, arrogance—the opposite—is treated as denial of God, as humility is the imitation of God.

Bavli Sotah 5B, XVI, XVII, XX–XXIII, XXIX

And R. Yohanan said in the name of R. Simeon b. Yohai, "Whoever is arrogant is as if he worships idolatry.

"Here it is written, 'Everyone who is arrogant in heart is an abomination to the Lord,' (Proverbs 16:5), and elsewhere it is written, 'You will not bring an abomination into your house' (Deuteronomy 7:26)."

And R. Yohanan on his own account said, "He is as if he denied the very Principle [of the world],

"as it is said, 'Your heart will be lifted up and you will forget the Lord your God' (Deuteronomy 8:14)."

R. Hama bar Hanina said, "He is as if he had sexual relations with all of those women forbidden to him on the laws of incest.

"Here it is written, 'Everyone who is arrogant in heart is an abomination to the Lord' (Proverbs 16:5), and elsewhere it is written, 'For all these abominations . . .' (Leviticus 18:27)."

Ulla said, "It is as if he built a high place,

"as it is said, 'Cease you from man, whose breath is in his nostrils, for wherein is he to be accounted of' (Isaiah 2:22).

"Do not read, 'wherein,' but rather, 'high place.' "

Whence [in Scripture] do we derive an admonition against the arrogant?

Said Raba said Zeiri, " 'Listen and give ear, do not be proud' (Jeremiah 13:15)."

R. Nahman bar Isaac said, "From the following: 'Your heart will be lifted up, and you will forget the Lord your God' (Deuteronomy 8:14).

"And it is written, 'Beware, lest you forget the Lord your God' (Deuteronomy 8:11)."

And that accords with what R. Abin said R. Ilaa said.

For R. Abin said R. Ilaa said, "In every place in which it is said, 'Beware lest . . . that you not . . . ,' the meaning is only to lay down a negative commandment [so that one who does such a thing violates a negative admonition]."

"With him also who is of a contrite and humble spirit" (Isaiah 57:15).
R. Huna and R. Hisda:
One said, "I [God] am with the contrite."
The other said, "I [God] am the contrite."
Logic favors the view of him who has said, "I [God] am with the contrite," for lo, the Holy One, blessed be he, neglected all mountains and heights and brought his Presence to rest on Mount Sinai,
and he did not raise Mount Sinai upward [to himself].
R. Joseph said, "A person should always learn from the attitude of his Creator, for lo, the Holy One, blessed be he, neglected all mountains and heights and brought his Presence to rest on Mount Sinai,
"and he neglected all valuable trees and brought his Presence to rest in the bush."

Said R. Eleazar, "Whoever is arrogant is worthy of being cut down like an *asherah* [a tree that is worshipped].
"Here it is written, 'The high ones of stature shall be cut down' (Isaiah 10:33),
"and elsewhere it is written, 'And you shall hew down their *asherim*' (Deuteronomy 7:5)."
And R. Eleazar said, "Whoever is arrogant—his dust will not be stirred up [in the resurrection of the dead].
"For it is said, 'Awake and sing, you that dwell in the dust' (Isaiah 26:19).
"It is stated not 'you who lie in the dust' but 'you who dwell in the dust,' meaning, one who has become a neighbor to the dust [by constant humility] even in his lifetime."
And R. Eleazar said, "For whoever is arrogant the Presence of God laments,
"as it is said, 'But the haughty he knows from afar' (Psalms 138:6)."

R. Avira expounded, and some say it was R. Eleazar, "Come and take note of the fact that not like the trait of the Holy One, blessed be he, is the trait of flesh and blood.

"The trait of flesh and blood is that those who are high take note of those who are high, but the one who is high does not take note of the one who is low.

"But the trait of the Holy One, blessed be he, is not that way. He is high, but he takes note of the low,

"as it is said, 'For though the Lord is high, yet he takes note of the low' (Psalms 138:6)."

Said R. Hisda, and some say it was Mar Uqba, "Concerning whoever is arrogant said the Holy One, blessed be he, he and I cannot live in the same world,

"as it is said, 'Whoever slanders his neighbor in secret—him will I destroy; him who has a haughty look and a proud heart I will not endure' (Psalms 101:5).

"Do not read, 'him [I cannot endure]' but 'with him [I cannot endure].'"

There are those who apply the foregoing teaching to those who slander, as it is said, "Whoever slanders his neighbor in secret—him will I destroy" (Psalms 101:5).

Said R. Joshua b. Levi, "Come and take note of how great are the humble in the sight of the Holy One, blessed be he.

"For when the sanctuary stood, a person would bring a burnt-offering, gaining thereby the reward for bringing a burnt-offering, or a meal-offering, and gaining the reward for a meal offering.

"But a person who is genuinely humble does Scripture treat as if he had made offerings of all the sacrifices,

"as it is said, 'The sacrifices [plural] of God are a broken spirit' (Psalms 51:19).

"And not only so, but his prayer is not rejected, as it is said, 'A broken and contrite heart, O God, you will not despise' (Psalms 51:19)."

The repertoire shows clearly that sages impute to God those traits of personality that are recommended and claim that God favors personalities like God's own. The clear implication is that God and the human being are consubstantial as to attitudes, emotions, and other aspects of virtue.

God laughs just as does a human being. The attribution to God of a sense of humor portrays the divinity once more as incarnate, the model by which the human being was made, not only in physical form but also in personality traits.

Bavli Baba Mesia 59A–B

There we have learned: If one cut [a clay oven] into parts and put sand between the parts,

R. Eliezer declares the oven broken-down and therefore insusceptible to uncleanness.

And sages declare it susceptible.

And this is what is meant by the oven of Akhnai [Mishnah *Qelim* 5:10].

Why the oven of Akhnai?

Said R. Judah said Samuel, "It is because they surrounded it with argument as with a snake and proved it was insusceptible to uncleanness."

It has been taught on Tannaite authority:

On that day R. Eliezer produced all of the arguments in the world, but they did not accept them from him. So he said to them, "If the law accords with my position, this carob tree will prove it."

The carob was uprooted from its place by a hundred cubits—and some say, four hundred cubits.

They said to him, "There is no proof from a carob tree."

So he went and said to them, "If the law accords with my position, let the stream of water prove it."

The stream of water reversed flow.

They said to him, "There is no proof from a stream of water."

So he went and said to them, "If the law accords with my position, let the walls of the school house prove it."

The walls of the school house tilted toward falling.

R. Joshua rebuked them, saying to them, "If disciples of sages are contending with one another in matters of law, what business do you have?"

They did not fall on account of the honor owing to R. Joshua, but they also did not straighten up on account of the honor owing to R. Eliezer, and to this day they are still tilted.

So he went and said to them, "If the law accords with my position, let the Heaven prove it!"

An echo came forth, saying, "What business have you with R. Eliezer, for the law accords with his position under all circumstances!"

R. Joshua stood up on his feet and said, " 'It is not in Heaven' (Deuteronomy 30:12)."

What is the sense of, " 'It is not in Heaven' (Deuteronomy 30:12)"?

Said R. Jeremiah, "[The sense of Joshua's statement is this:] For the

Torah has already been given from Mount Sinai, so we do not pay attention to echoes, since you have already written in the Torah at Mount Sinai, 'After the majority you are to incline' (Exodus 23:2)."

R. Nathan came upon Elijah and said to him, "What did the Holy One, blessed be he, do at that moment?"

He said to him, "He laughed and said, 'My children have overcome me, my children have overcome me!' "

They said:

On that day they brought all of the objects that R. Eliezer had declared insusceptible to uncleanness and burned them in fire [as though they were unclean beyond all purification].

They furthermore took a vote against him and cursed him.

They said, "Who will go and inform him?"

Said to them R. Akiva, "I shall go and tell him, lest someone unworthy go and tell him, and he turn out to destroy the entire world [with his curse]."

What did R. Akiva do? He put on black garments and cloaked himself in a black cloak and took his seat before him at a distance of four cubits.

Said to him R. Eliezer, "Akiva, why is today different from all other days?"

He said to him, "My lord, it appears to me that your colleagues are keeping distance from you."

Then he too tore his garments and removed his shoes, moved his stool and sat down on the ground, with tears streaming from his eyes.

The world was blighted: a third olives, a third wheat, a third barley.

And some say, also the dough in women's hands swelled up.

A Tanna taught:

There was a great disaster that day, for every place upon which R. Eliezer set his eyes was burned up.

And also Rabban Gamaliel was coming by ship. A big wave arose to drown him.

He said, "It appears to me that this is on account only of R. Eliezer b. Hyrcanus."

He stood upon his feet and said, "Lord of the world, it is perfectly obvious to you that it was not for my own honor that I have acted, nor for the honor of the house of my father have I acted, but it was for the honor owing to you, specifically, so that dissension should not become rife in Israel."

The sea subsided.

Imma Shalom, the wife of R. Eliezer, was the sister of Rabban Gamaliel. From that time onward she never left R. Eliezer to fall on his face [in prayer]. [So great was the power of his prayer that if he were to recite certain prayers because of the injury done him, God would listen and destroy her brother.]

One day, which was the day of the New Moon, she mistook, assuming that the month was a defective one; and others say, she was distracted by a poor man who came and stood at her door, and to whom she took out a piece of bread.

She found that her husband had fallen on his face, and she said to him, "Get up, for you have killed my brother."

Meanwhile the word came from the house of Rabban Gamaliel that he had died.

He said to her, "Then how did you know?"

She said to him, "So do I have as a tradition from the household of the father of my father: 'All gates are locked, except for the gates that receive complaints against overreaching.' "

God's laughter is not only because of delight. It may also take on a sardonic character, for instance, as ridicule.

Bavli Abodah Zarah

Said R. Yose, "In the age to come idolators will come and convert [to Judaism] . . . and will put phylacteries on their foreheads and arms, place show-fringes on their garments and a *mezuzah* on their doorposts. When, however, the battle of Gog and Magog takes place, they will be asked, 'Why have you come?'

"They will reply, 'Against God and his anointed . . .' (Psalms 2:1).

"Then each of the converts will toss off the religious emblems and leave . . . and the Holy One, blessed be he, will sit and laugh,

"as it is said, 'He who sits in heaven laughs . . .' (Psalms 2:4)."

The repertoire of God's emotions encompasses not only desirable, but also undesirable traits. God not only exhibits and favors humility and has the capacity to laugh out of both joy and ridicule, God also becomes angry and acts to express that anger:

Bavli Berakhot 7A, LI

And said R. Yohanan in the name of R. Yose, "How do we know that one should not placate a person when he is angry?

"It is in line with the following verse of Scripture: 'My face will go and then I will give you rest' (Exodus 33:14).

"Said the Holy One, blessed be he, to Moses, 'Wait until my angry countenance passes, and then I shall give you rest.' "

But does the Holy One, blessed be he, get angry?

Indeed so.

For it has been taught on Tannaite authority:

"A God that is angry every day" (Psalms 7:12).

And how long is this anger going to last?

A moment.

And how long is a moment?

It is one fifty-eight thousand eight hundred and eighty-eighth part of an hour.

And no creature except for the wicked Balaam has ever been able to fix the moment exactly.

For concerning him it has been written, "He knows the knowledge of the Most High" (Numbers 24:16).

Now if Balaam did not even know what his beast was thinking, was he likely to know what the Most High is thinking?

But this teaches that he knew exactly how to reckon the very moment that the Holy One, blessed be he, would be angry.

That is in line with what the prophet said to Israel, "O my people, remember now what Balak, king of Moab, devised, and what Balaam, son of Beor, answered him . . . that you may know the righteous acts of the Lord" (Micah 6:5).

Said R. Eleazar, "The Holy One, blessed be he, said to Israel, 'Know that I did any number of acts of righteousness with you, for I did not get angry in the time of the wicked Balaam. For had I gotten angry, not one of (the enemies of) Israel would have survived, not a remnant.'

"That is in line with what Balaam said to Balak, 'How shall I curse whom God has not cursed, and how shall I execrate whom the Lord has not execrated?' (Numbers 23:8).

"This teaches that for that entire time [God] did not get mad."

And how long is God's anger?

It is a moment.

And how long is a moment?

Said R. Abin, and some say, R. Abina, "A moment lasts as long as it takes to say 'a moment.' "

And how do we know that a moment is how long God is angry?

For it is said, "For his anger is but for a moment, his favor is for a lifetime" (Psalms 30:6).

If you like, you may derive the lesson from the following: "Hide yourself for a little while until the anger be past" (Isaiah 26:20).

And when is God angry?

Said Abayye, "It is during the first three hours of the day, when the comb of the cock is white, and it stands on one foot."

But it stands on one foot every hour.

To be sure, it stands on its foot every hour, but in all the others it has red streaks, and in the moment at hand there are no red streaks [in the comb of the cock].

What is striking in this sizable account is the characterization of God's anger in entirely corporeal terms. God not only becomes angry, God also acts in anger. For one example, in anger God loses his temper.

Bavli Baba Batra 74B

Said R. Judah said Rab, "When the Holy One, blessed be he, proposed to create the world, he said to the angelic prince of the sea, 'Open your mouth and swallow all the water in the world.'

"He said to him, 'Lord of the world, it is quite sufficient if I stick with what I already have.'

"Forthwith he kicked him with his foot and killed him.

"For it is written, 'He stirs up the sea with his power, and by his understanding he smites through Rahab' (Job 26:12)."

Like a human being, God thus can lose his temper. God's anger derives not only from ill temper but from deeper causes. God is dissatisfied with the world as it is and so expresses anger with the present condition of humanity, on account of Israel.

Bavli Berakhot 3A, VI–VIII

For it has been taught on Tannaite authority:

R. Eliezer says, "The night is divided into three watches, and [in heaven] over each watch the Holy One, blessed be he, sits and roars like a lion,

"as it is said, 'The Lord roars from on high and raises his voice from his holy habitation, roaring he does roar because of his fold' (Jeremiah 25:30).

"The indication of each watch is as follows: at the first watch, an ass brays, at the second, dogs yelp, at the third, an infant sucks at its mother's breast or a woman whispers to her husband."

Said R. Isaac bar Samuel in the name of Rab, "The night is divided into three watches, and over each watch, The Holy One, blessed be he, sits and roars like a lion.

"He says, 'Woe to the children, on account of whose sins I have wiped out my house and burned my palace, and whom I have exiled among the nations of the world.' "

It has been taught on Tannaite authority:

Said R. Yose, "Once I was going along the way, and I went into one of the ruins of Jerusalem to pray. Elijah, of blessed memory, came and watched over me at the door until I had finished my prayer. After I had finished my prayer, he said to me, 'Peace be to you, my lord.'

"And I said to him, 'Peace be to you, my lord and teacher.'

"And he said to me, 'My son, on what account did you go into this ruin?'

"And I said to him, 'To pray.'

"And he said to me, 'You would have done better to pray on the road.'

"And he said to me, 'My son, what sound did you hear in this ruin?'

"I said to him, 'I heard the sound of an echo moaning like a pigeon and saying, "Woe to the children, on account of whose sins I have wiped out my house and burned my palace and whom I have exiled among the nations of the world." '

"He said to me, 'By your life and the life of your head, it is not only at this moment that the echo speaks in such a way, but three times daily, it says the same thing.

" 'And not only so, but when Israelites go into synagogues and schoolhouses and respond, "May the great name be blessed," the Holy One shakes his head and says, "Happy is the king, whom they praise in his house in such a way! What does a father have, who has exiled his children? And woe to the children who are exiled from their father's table!" ' "

God's anger and mourning form emotions identical to those of human beings, as is made explicit. Israel are God's children, and

God mourns for them as a parent mourns for children who have suffered. The personality of God therefore takes the form of these attitudes, as the same as those of human beings, though of a cosmic order. But God's anger derives from broader causes than Israel's current condition.

The humanity of God emerges in yet another way. God enters into transactions with human beings and accords with the rules that govern those relationships. So God exhibits precisely the social attributes that human beings do. A number of stories, rather protracted and detailed, tell the story of God as a social being, living among and doing business with mortals. These stories provide extended portraits of God's relationships, in particular arguments, with important figures, such as angelic figures, as well as Moses, David, and Hosea. In them God negotiates, persuades, teaches, argues, exchanges, reasons. The personality of God therefore comes to expression in a variety of portraits of how God engages in such arguments and so enters into the existence of ordinary people. These disputes, negotiations, and transactions yield a portrait of God who is reasonable and capable of give and take, as in the following:

Bavli Arakhin 15A-B

Rabbah bar Mari said, "What is the meaning of this verse: 'But they were rebellious at the sea, even at the Red Sea; nonetheless he saved them for his name's sake' (Psalms 106:7)?

"This teaches that the Israelites were rebellious at that time, saying, 'Just as we will go up on this side, so the Egyptians will go up on the other side.' Said the Holy One, blessed be he, to the angelic prince who reigns over the sea, 'Cast them [the Israelites] out on dry land.'

"He said before him, 'Lord of the world, is there any case of a slave [namely, myself] to whom his master [you] gives a gift [the Israelites], and then the master goes and takes [the gift] away again? [You gave me the Israelites, now you want to take them away and place them on dry land.]'

"He said to him, 'I'll give you one and a half times their number.'

"He said before him, 'Lord of the world, is there a possibility that a slave can claim anything against his master? [How do I know that you will really do it?]'

"He said to him, 'The Kishon brook will be my pledge [that I shall carry out my word. Nine hundred chariots at the brook were sunk, (Judges 3:23) while Pharaoh at the sea had only six hundred, thus a pledge one and a half times greater than the sum at issue.]'

"Forthwith [the angelic prince of the sea] spit them out onto dry land, for it is written, 'And the Israelites saw the Egyptians dead on the sea shore' (Exodus 14:30)."

God is willing to give a pledge to guarantee his word. He furthermore sees the right claim of the counterpart actor in the story. Hence we see how God obeys precisely the same social laws of exchange and reason that govern other incarnate beings.

Still more interesting is the picture of God's argument with Abraham. God is represented as accepting accountability, by the standards of humanity, for what God does.

Bavli Menahot 53B

Said R. Isaac, "When the temple was destroyed, the Holy One, blessed be he, found Abraham standing in the Temple. He said to him, 'What is my beloved doing in my house?'

"He said to him, 'I have come because of what is going on with my children.'

"He said to him, 'Your children sinned and have been sent into exile.'

"He said to him, 'But wasn't it by mistake that they sinned?'

"He said to him, 'She has wrought lewdness' (Jeremiah 11:15).

"He said to him, 'But wasn't it just a minority of them that did it?'

"He said to him, 'It was a majority' (Jeremiah 11:15).

"He said to him, 'You should at least have taken account of the covenant of circumcision [which should have secured forgiveness despite their sin]!'

"He said to him, 'The holy flesh is passed from you' (Jeremiah 11:15).

" 'And if you had waited for them, they might have repented!'

"He said to him, 'When you do evil, then you are happy' (Jeremiah 11:15).

"He said to him, 'He put his hands on his head, crying out and weeping, saying to them, God forbid! Perhaps they have no remedy at all!'

"A heavenly voice came forth and said, 'The Lord called you "a leafy olive tree, fair with excellent fruit" ' (Jeremiah 11:16).

" 'Just as in the case of an olive tree, its future comes only at the end [that is, it is only after a long while that it attains its best fruit], so in the case of Israel, their future comes at the end of their time.' "

God relates to Abraham as to an equal. That is shown by God's implicit agreement that he is answerable to Abraham for what has taken place with the destruction of the Temple. God does not impose on Abraham silence, saying that that is a decree not to be contested but only accepted. God as a social being accepts that he must provide sound reasons for his actions, as must any other reasonable person in a world governed by rules applicable to everyone. Abraham is a fine choice for the protagonist, since he engaged in the argument concerning Sodom. His complaint is expressed in the second paragraph above: God is now called to explain himself. At each point then Abraham offers arguments in behalf of sinning Israel, and God responds, item by item. The climax, of course, has God promising Israel a future worth having. God emerges as both just and merciful, reasonable but sympathetic. The transaction attests to God's conformity to rules of reasoned transactions in a coherent society.

The same picture is drawn in still greater detail when God engages Hosea in discussion. Here, however, Hosea complains against Israel and God takes the part of Abraham in the earlier account. God's social role is defined in the model of the sage or master, a role we shall presently find prominent in the repertoire of portraits of personality. God teaches Hosea by providing him with an analogy of what Hosea proposes that God do.

Bavli Pesahim 87A

Said the Holy One, blessed be he, to Hosea, "Your children have sinned."

He should have said to him, "They are your children, children of those to whom you have shown grace, children of Abraham, Isaac, and Jacob. Send your mercy to them."

It is not enough that he did not say the right thing, but he said to him, "Lord of the world, the entire world is yours. Trade them in for some other nation."

Said the Holy One, blessed be he, "What shall I then do with that elder? I shall tell him, 'Go, marry a whore and have children of prostitution.' Then I'll tell him, 'Divorce her.' If he can send her away, then I'll send away Israel."

For it is said, "And the Lord said to Hosea, Go, take a whore and have children of prostitution" (Hosea 1:1).

After he had two sons and a daughter, the Holy One, blessed be he, said to Hosea, "Should you not have learned the lesson of your master, Moses? Once I had entered into discourse with him, he separated from his wife. So you too, take your leave of her."

He said to him, "Lord of the world, I have children from her, and I simply cannot drive her out or divorce her."

Said to him the Holy One, blessed be he, "Now if you, married to a whore, with children of prostitution, and you don't even know whether they're yours or whether they come from some other fathers, are in such a state, as to Israel, who are my children, children of those whom I have tested, the children of Abraham, Isaac and Jacob . . .

". . . how can you say to me, 'Trade them in for some other nation'?"

When [Hosea] realized that he had sinned, he arose to seek mercy for himself. Said the Holy One, blessed be he, to him, "Instead of seeking mercy for yourself, seek mercy for Israel, against whom I have on your account issued three decrees [exile, rejection, and without compassion, reflecting the names of his children]."

He went and sought mercy and [God] annulled [the decrees] and gave them this blessing: "Yet the number of the children of Israel shall be as the sand of the sea . . . and instead of being called 'You are not my people,' they will be called 'You are the children of the living God.' And the children of Judah and the children of Israel shall be gathered together . . . And I will sow her to me in the land, and have compassion on her who was not treated with compassion and say to those who were not my people, 'You are my people' (Hosea 2:1-2, 2:25)."

Hosea negotiates with God, proposing that God reject Israel for some other nation. God's reply is that of an experienced teacher. He puts the disciple through a concrete lesson, which imparts to the disciple the desired experience and leads to the disciple's drawing the right conclusion. The social transaction then is worked out in accord with rules of reason. Just as experience teaches Hosea the lesson that one does not reject, but forgives, sinful relations, so

Hosea draws the correct conclusion. The story then portrays God in a social transaction that is governed by accepted laws of orderly conduct.

God's relationships with David, a paramount theme in the story of David's sin with Bath Sheba, yield the picture of how God responds in a reasonable way to a reasonable proposal. Then, to be sure, God teaches a lesson of right conduct, but, throughout, God's role remains the same: a social and rational being, like mortals. What is important for my argument is the representation of God as engaged in negotiation in accord with rules that apply to heaven and earth alike. God enters into society as a full participant in the world of humanity and plays a role that is the counterpart to that of any just person. The personality of God here takes the now well-established form of God as fully engaged in social transactions with counterparts on earth. We consider only those portions of the protracted story that pertain to our topic:

Bavli Sanhedrin 106B–107A, CCXLVI-CCLI

Said R. Judah said Rab, "One should never put himself to the test, for lo, David, king of Israel, put himself to the test and he stumbled.

"He said before him, 'Lord of the world, on what account do people say, "God of Abraham, God of Isaac, and God of Jacob," but they do not say, "God of David"?'

"He said to him, 'They endured a test for me, while you have not endured a test for me.'

"He said before him, 'Lord of the world, here I am. Test me.'

"For it is said, 'Examine me, O Lord, and try me' (Psalms 26:1).

"He said to him, 'I shall test you, and I shall do for you something that I did not do for them. I did not inform them [what I was doing], while I shall tell you what I am going to do. I shall try you with a matter having to do with sexual relations.'

"Forthwith: 'And it came to pass in an eventide that David arose from off his bed' (2 Samuel 11:2)."

The opening passage represents God in conversation with David and responsive to David's reasoning. This is more than the presence of God familiar in the earliest strata of the canon, God in conversation with David forms a personality, not the mere "You" of prayer familiar in the initial writings of the Judaism of the Dual Torah. Where God cites Scripture, it is not merely to prove a point but to make a statement particular to the exchange at hand. So this is not a conventional portrait of God's serving as the voice of an established text, but rather the picture of God engaged in a social transaction with a sentient being.

We skip the description of David's relationship with Bath Sheba and move directly to David's plea of forgiveness. In the passages that follow, God serves merely as audience for David's statements:

Raba interpreted Scripture, asking, "What is the meaning of the following verse: 'To the chief musician, a Psalm of David. In the Lord I put my trust, how do you say to my soul, Flee as a bird to your mountain?' (Psalms 11:1)?

"Said David before the Holy One, blessed be he, 'Lord of the world, Forgive me for that sin, so that people should not say, "The mountain that is among you [that is, your king] has been driven off by a bird." ' "

Raba interpreted Scripture, asking, "What is the meaning of the following verse: 'Against you, you alone, have I sinned, and done this evil in your sight, that you might be justified when you speak and be clear when you judge' (Psalms 11:1)?

"Said David before the Holy One, blessed be he, 'Lord of the world. It is perfectly clear to you that if I had wanted to overcome my impulse to do evil, I should have done so. But I had in mind that people not say, "The slave has conquered the Master [God, and should then be included as 'God of David']." ' "

Raba interpreted Scripture, asking, "What is the meaning of the following verse: 'For I am ready to halt and my sorrow is continually before me' (Psalms 38:18)?

"Bath Sheba, daughter of Eliam, was designated for David from the six days of creation, but she came to him through anguish."

And so did a Tannaite authority of the house of R. Ishmael [teach], "Bath Sheba, daughter of Eliam, was designated for David, but he 'ate' her while she was yet unripe."

Raba interpreted Scripture, asking, "What is the meaning of the following verse: 'But in my adversity they rejoiced and gathered themselves together, yes, the abjects gathered themselves together against me and I did not know it, they tore me and did not cease' (Psalms 35:15)?

"Said David before the Holy One, blessed be he, 'Lord of the world, it is perfectly clear to you that if they had torn my flesh, my blood would not have flowed [because I was so embarrassed].

" 'Not only so, but when they take up the four modes of execution inflicted by a court, they interrupt their Mishnah study and say to me, "David, he who has sexual relations with a married woman—how is he put to death?"

" 'I say to them, "He who has sexual relations with a married woman is put to death through strangulation, but he has a share in the world to come," while he who humiliates his fellow in public has no share in the world to come.' "

Now God emerges once more and plays the role of antagonist to David's protagonist:

R. Dosetai of Biri interpreted Scripture, "To what may David be likened? To a gentile merchant.

"Said David before the Holy One, blessed be he, 'Lord of the world, "Who can understand his errors?" (Psalms 19:13).'

"He said to him, 'They are remitted for you.'

" ' "Cleanse me of hidden faults" (Psalms 19:13).'

" 'They are remitted to you.'

" ' "Keep back your servant also from presumptuous sins" (Psalms 19:14).'

" 'They are remitted to you.'

" ' "Let them not have dominion over me, then I shall be upright" (Psalms 19:14), so that the rabbis will not hold me up as an example.'

" 'They are remitted to you.'

" ' "And I shall be innocent of great transgression" (Psalms 19:14), so that they will not write down my ruin.'

"He said to him, 'That is not possible. Now if the Y that I took away from the name of Saray [changing it from Saray to Sarah] stood crying for so many years until Joshua came and I added the Y [removed from Sarah's name] to his name, as it is said, "And Moses called Oshea, the son of Nun, Jehoshua" (Numbers 13:16), how much the more will a complete passage of Scripture [cry out if I remove that passage from its rightful place]!' "

God once more emerges as a fully formed personality, for God's role here is not merely to cite Scripture. God can do just so much, but no more, and this detail is the contribution not of Scripture but of the storyteller. The personality of God once more takes shape in the notion of God as bound by rules of procedure and conduct. God enters into civil and rational transactions with human beings and conforms to these rules, with the result that is expressed here.

"And I shall be innocent from great transgression": (Psalms 19:14):
He said before him, "Lord of the world, forgive me for the whole of that sin [as though I had never done it]."
He said to him, "Solomon, your son, even now is destined to say in his wisdom, 'Can a man take fire in his bosom, and his clothes not be burned? Can one go upon hot coals, and his feet not be burned? So he who goes in to his neighbor's wife, whoever touches her shall not be innocent' (Proverbs 6:27–29)."
He said to him, "Will I be so deeply troubled?"
He said to him, "Accept suffering [as atonement]."
He accepted the suffering.

Said R. Judah said Rab, "For six months David was afflicted with *saraat*, and the Presence of God left him, and the sanhedrin abandoned him.
"He was afflicted with *saraat*, as it is written, 'Purge me with hyssop and I shall be clean, wash me and I shall be whiter than snow' (Psalms 51:9).
"The Presence of God left him, as it is written, 'Restore to me the joy of your salvation and uphold me with your free spirit' (Psalms 51:14).
"The sanhedrin abandoned him, as it is written, 'Let those who fear you turn to me and those who have known your testimonies' (Psalms 119:79).
"How do we know that this lasted for six months? As it is written, 'And the days that David ruled over Israel were forty years: Seven years he reigned in Hebron, and thirty-three years he reigned in Jerusalem' (I Kings 2:11).
"Elsewhere it is written, 'In Hebron he reigned over Judah seven years and six months' (2 Samuel 5:5).
"So the six months were not taken into account. Accordingly, he was afflicted with *saraat* [for such a one is regarded as a corpse].
"He said before him, 'Lord of the world, forgive me for that sin.'
" 'It is forgiven to you.'
" ' "Then show me a token for good, that they who hate me may see it and be ashamed, because you, Lord, have helped me and comforted me" (Psalms 86:17).'

"He said to him, 'While you are alive, I shall not reveal [the fact that you are forgiven], but I shall reveal it in the lifetime of your son, Solomon.'

"When Solomon had built the house of the sanctuary, he tried to bring the ark into the house of the Holy of Holies. The gates cleaved to one another. He recited twenty-four prayers[2] but was not answered.

"He said, 'Lift up your head, O you gates, and be lifted up, you everlasting doors, and the King of glory shall come in. Who is this King of glory? The Lord strong and mighty, the Lord mighty in battle' (Psalms 24:7ff.).

"And it is further said, 'Lift up your heads, O you gates even lift them up, you everlasting doors' (Psalms 24:7).

"But he was not answered.

"When he said, 'Lord God, turn not away the face of your anointed, remember the mercies of David, your servant' (2 Chronicles 6:42), forthwith he was answered.

"At that moment the faces of David's enemies turned as black as the bottom of a pot, for all Israel knew that the Holy One, blessed be he, had forgiven him for that sin."

As we see, our hero is not God but David. The story is not told to characterize God, who plays a supporting part, if not a mere straight man. Nonetheless, the portrayal of God justifies the claim that we have here an incarnate God, consubstantial with humanity not only in physical and emotional traits, but even more so in the conformity to the social laws of correct transactions that, in theory at least, make society possible.

Among the available models for the personality of God—warrior, teacher, young man—the one that predominated entailed representation of God as sage. God is represented as a school master:

Bavli Abodah Zarah 3B

"He sits and teaches school children, as it is said, 'Whom shall one teach knowledge, and whom shall one make to understand the message? Those who are weaned from milk' (Isaiah 28:9)."

---

[2]Freedman, *The Babylonian Talmud,* p. 734, n. 4: in 2 Chronicles 6, words for prayer, supplication, and hymn occur twenty-four times.

But this is not the same thing as God as a master-sage teaching mature disciples, that is, God as rabbi and sage. That representation emerges in a variety of ways and proves the single most important mode of the personality of God. God's personality merged throughout with the Bavli's authorships' representation of the personality of the ideal master or sage. That representation in the Bavli proved detailed and specific. A sage's life—Torah learned, then taught, through discipleship—encompassed both the correct modes of discourse and ritual argument, on the one side, and the recasting of all relationships in accord with received convention of courtesy and subservience. God then is represented in both dimensions, as a master requiring correct conduct of his disciples, and as a teacher able to hold his own in arguments conducted in accord with the prevailing ritual. For one example, a master had the right to demand an appropriate greeting, and God, not receiving that greeting, asked why:

Bavli Shabbat 89A

Said R. Joshua b. Levi, "When Moses came up on high, he found the Holy One, blessed be he, tying crowns onto the letters of the Torah. He said to him, 'Moses, don't people say hello in your town?'

"He said to him, 'Does a servant greet his master [first]?'

"He said to him, 'You should have helped me [at least by greeting me and wishing me success].'

"He said to him, ' "Now I pray you let the power of the Lord be great, just as you have said" (Numbers 14:17).' "

Moses here plays the role of disciple to God the teacher, a persistent pattern throughout. Not having offered the appropriate greeting, the hapless disciple is instructed on the matter. Part of the ritual of "being a sage" thus comes to expression.

Yet another detail of that same ritual taught how to make a request—and how not to do so. A request offered in humility is proper; one made in an arrogant or demanding spirit is not. Knowing what to ask is as important as knowing how. The congregation of Israel shows how not to do so, and God shows, nonetheless, the right mode of response.

Bavli Taanit 4A

The congregation of Israel made its request in an improper way, but the Holy One, blessed be he, responded in a proper way.

For it is said, [the congregation of Israel said to God,] "And let us know, eagerly strive to know, the Lord, the Lord's going forth is sure as the morning, and the Lord shall come to us as the rain" (Hosea 6:3).

Said the Holy One, blessed be he, to [the congregation of Israel,] "My daughter, now you are asking for something which sometimes is wanted and sometimes is not really wanted. But I shall give you something which is always wanted.

"For it is said, 'I will be as dew to Israel' (Hosea 14:6)."

Further, [the congregation of Israel] made its request in an improper manner, "O God, set me as a seal on your heart, as a seal on your arm" (Song of Songs 8:6).

[But the Holy One, blessed be he, responded in a proper way.] Said the Holy One, blessed be he, to [the congregation of Israel,] "My daughter, now you are asking for something which sometimes can be seen and sometimes cannot be seen. But I shall give you something which can always be seen.

"For it is said, 'Behold, I have graven you on the palms of my hands' (Isaiah 49:16) [and the palms are always visible, in a way in which the heart and arm are not]."

Dew is always wanted, rain not. To be a seal on the heart or arm is to be displayed only occasionally, but the hands are always visible. Consequently, God as sage teaches Israel as disciple how to make a proper request.

The status of sage, expressed in rituals of proper conduct, is attained through knowing how to participate in argument about matters of the Torah, particularly the law. Indeed, what makes a sage an authority is knowledge of details of the law. Consequently, my claim that God is represented as a particular sort of human being, namely, as a sage, requires evidence that God not only follows the arguments (as above, "My sons have conquered me!") and even has opinions which he proposes to interject, but also himself participates in debates on the law. Ability to follow those debates and forcefully contribute to them forms the chief indicator. That that ability joins some men to God is furthermore explicit. So the arguments in the academy in Heaven, over which God presides, form the exact counterpart to the arguments on earth, with the result that God emerges as precisely consubstantial, physically and intellectually, with the particular configuration of the sage:

Bavli Baba Mesia 86A

In the session in the firmament, people were debating this question: if the bright spot came before the white hair, the person is unclean. If the white hair came before the bright spot, he is clean. What about a case of doubt?

The Holy One, blessed be he, said, "Clean."

And the rest of the fellowship of the firmament said, "Unclean."

They said, "Who will settle the matter?"

It should be Rabbah b. Nahmani, for he is the one who said, "I am an expert in the laws of plagues and in the effects of contamination through the overshadowing of a corpse." . . .

A letter fell down from the sky to Pumbedita: "Rabbah b. Nahmani has been called up by the academy of the firmament. . . ."

God in this story forms part of the background of action. The story, part of a much longer account attached to the academy of Pumbedita of how Rabbah b. Nahmani was taken up to Heaven, shows us how God is represented in a heavenly session of the heavenly academy studying precisely those details of the Torah, here Leviticus Chapter 13 as restated in Mishnah tractate *Negaim,* as were mastered by the great sages of the day. That the rest of the heavenly court would disagree forms an essential detail, because it verifies the picture and validates the claim, to come, that Heaven required the knowledge of the heroic sage. That is the point of the third to fifth paragraphs in the preceding extract. Then Rabbah b. Nahmani is called to Heaven—that is, killed and transported upward—to make the required ruling. God is not the centerpiece of the story. The detail that a letter was sent from the heavenly academy to the one on earth, at Pumbedita, then restates the basic point of the story, the correspondence of earth to Heaven on just this matter.

Though God is in the image of the sage, God towers over other sages, disposes of their lives, and determines their destinies. Por-

traying God as sage allowed the storytellers to state in a vivid way
their convictions on the disparity between sages' great intellectual
achievements and their this-worldly standing and fate. But God
remains within the model of other sages, takes up the rulings,
follows the arguments, and participates in the sessions that distinguish sages and mark them off from all other people:

Bavli Menahot 29B

Said R. Judah said Rab, "When Moses went up to the height, he found
the Holy One, blessed be he, sitting and tying crowns to the letters [of the
Torah]."

"He said to him, 'Lord of the universe, why is this necessary?'

"He said to him, 'There is a certain man who is going to come into
being at the end of some generations, by the name of Akiva b. Joseph. He
is going to find expositions to attach mounds and mounds of laws to each
point [of a crown].'

"He said to him, 'Lord of the universe, show him to me.'

"He said to him, 'Turn around.'

"[Moses] went and took his seat at the end of eight rows, but he could
not understand what the people were saying. He felt weak. When
discourse came to a certain matter, one of [Akiva's] disciples said to him,
'My lord, how do you know this?'

"He said to him, 'It is a law revealed by God to Moses at Mount Sinai.'

"Moses spirits were restored.

"He turned back and returned to the Holy One, blessed be he. He said
to him, 'Lord of the universe, now if you have such a man available, how
can you give the Torah through me?'

"He said to him, 'Be silent. That is how I have decided matters.'

"He said to him, 'Lord of the universe, you have now shown me his
mastery of the Torah. Now show me his reward.'

"He said to him, 'Turn around.'

"He turned around and saw people weighing out his flesh in the
butcher shop.

"He said to him, 'Lord of the universe, such is his mastery of Torah,
and such is his reward?'

"He said to him, 'Be silent. That is how I have decided matters.' "

This is the single most important narrative in the Bavli's repertoire
of allusions to and stories about the personality of God, for God's

role in the story finds definition as hero and principal actor. He is no longer the mere interlocutor, nor does he simply answer questions of the principal voice by citing Scripture. Quite to the contrary, God makes all the decisions and guides the unfolding of the story. Moses then appears as the straight man. He asks the questions that permit God to make the stunning replies. Why do you need crowns on the letters of the Torah? Akiva will explain them, by tying laws to these trivial and opaque details. What are these laws? I cannot follow them. Akiva will nonetheless attribute them to you. Why then give the Torah through me instead of him, since he understands it and I do not? It is my decree. Finally, comes the climax: what will this man's reward be? His flesh will be weighed out in butcher shops. The response remains the same. Moses, who is called "our rabbi" and forms the prototype and ideal of the sage, does not understand. God then tells him to shut up and accept his decree. God does what he likes, with whom he likes. Perhaps the storyteller had in mind a polemic against rebellious brilliance, as against dumb subservience. But that does not seem to me the urgent message, which rather requires acceptance of God's decrees, whatever they are—even when the undeserving receive glory, even when the accomplished come to nothing. The fact that God emerges as a fully formed personality—the model for the sage—hardly requires restatement.

Just as Israel glorifies God, so God responds and celebrates Israel. In the passages at hand, the complete personality of God, in physical, emotional, and social traits, comes to expression. God wears phylacteries, an indication of a corporeal sort. God further forms the correct attitude toward Israel, which is one of love, an indication of an attitude on the part of divinity corresponding to right attitudes on the part of human beings. Finally, to close the circle, just as there is a "you" to whom humanity prays, so God too says prayers—to God—and the point of these prayers is that God should elicit from himself forgiveness for Israel.

Bavli Berakhot 6A-B xxxix, 7A xlix, l

Said R. Nahman bar Isaac to R. Hiyya bar Abin, "As to the phylacteries of the Lord of the world, what is written in them?"

He said to him, " 'And who is like your people Israel, a singular nation on earth' (1 Chronicles 17:21)."

"And does the Holy One, blessed be he, sing praises for Israel?"

"Yes, for it is written, 'You have avouched the Lord this day . . . and the Lord has avouched you this day' (Deuteronomy 26:17, 18).

"Said the Holy One, blessed be he, to Israel, 'You have made me a singular entity in the world, and I shall make you a singular entity in the world.

" 'You have made me a singular entity in the world,' as it is said, 'Hear O Israel, the Lord, our God, the Lord is one' (Deuteronomy 6:4).

" 'And I shall make you a singular entity in the world,' as it is said, 'And who is like your people, Israel, a singular nation in the earth' (1 Chronicles 17:21)."

Said R. Aha, son of Raba to R. Ashi, "That takes care of one of the four subdivisions of the phylactery. What is written in the others?"

He said to him, " 'For what great nation is there . . . And what great nation is there . . .' (Deuteronomy 4:7, 8), 'Happy are you, O Israel . . .' (Deuteronomy 33:29), 'Or has God tried . . . ,' (Deuteronomy 4:34). And 'To make you high above all nations' (Deuteronomy 26:19)."

"If so, there are too many boxes!

"But the verses, 'For what great nation is there' and 'And what great nation is there,' which are equivalent, are in one box, and 'Happy are you, O Israel' and 'Who is like your people Israel' are in one box, and 'Or has God tried . . . ,' in one box, and 'To make you high' in one box.

"And all of them are written in the phylactery that is on the arm."

Said R. Yohanan in the name of R. Yose, "How do we know that the Holy One, blessed be he, says prayers?

"Since it is said, 'Even them will I bring to my holy mountain and make them joyful in my house of prayer' (Isaiah 56:7).

" 'Their house of prayer' is not stated, but rather, 'my house of prayer.'

"On the basis of that usage we see that the Holy One, blessed be he, says prayers."

What prayers does he say?

Said R. Zutra bar Tobiah said Rab, " 'May it be my will that my mercy overcome my anger, and that my mercy prevail over my attributes, so that I may treat my children in accord with the trait of mercy and in their regard go beyond the strict measure of the law.' "

It has been taught on Tannaite authority:

Said R. Ishmael b. Elisha, "One time I went in to offer up incense on the innermost altar, and I saw the crown of the Lord, enthroned on the highest throne, and he said to me, 'Ishmael, my son, bless me.'

"I said to him, 'May it be your will that your mercy overcome your anger, and that your mercy prevail over your attributes, so that you treat your children in accord with the trait of mercy and in their regard go beyond the strict measure of the law.'

"And he nodded his head to me."

And from that story we learn that the blessing of a common person should not be negligible in your view.

The corporeal side to the personality of God is clear at the outset: God's wearing phylacteries. The consubstantial traits of attitude and feeling—just as humanity feels joy, so does God; just as humanity celebrates God, so does God celebrate Israel—are made explicit. The social transactions of personality are specified as well. Just as Israel declares God to be unique, so God declares Israel to be unique. And just as Israel prays to God, so God says prayers. What God asks of God is that God transcend God—which is what, in prayer, humanity asks for as well. In the end, therefore, to be "in our image, after our likeness," the power of the powerless, the riches of the disinherited, the valuation and valorization of the will of those who have no right to will, is to be not the mirror image of God but very much like God.

INDEX

About the Author

Jacob Neusner is Graduate Research Professor of Religious Studies at the University of South Florida. The recipient of numerous scholarships, fellowships, awards, and research grants, Dr. Neusner is the author or editor of 385 books, including *The Mishnah: An Introduction* and *The Midrash: An Introduction*. Dr. Neusner holds twelve honorary degrees and medals and has lectured throughout the world.